# Other Books in This Series

Balanced Sourcing: Cooperation and Competition
in Supplier Relationships
*Timothy M. Laseter*

Smart Alliances: A Practical Guide to Repeatable Success
*John R. Harbison, Peter Pekar Jr.*

Thought Leaders: Insights on the Future of Business
*Joel Kurtzman, Editor*

# Channel Champions

# CHANNEL

A *Strategy & Business* Book
Booz·Allen & Hamilton

# CHAMPIONS

## How Leading Companies Build New Strategies to Serve Customers

Steven Wheeler • Evan Hirsh

Foreword by William F. Stasior

Jossey-Bass Publishers
San Francisco

Jossey-Bass books and products are available through most bookstores. To contact Jossey-Bass directly, call (888) 378–2537, fax to (800) 605–2665, or visit our website at www.josseybass.com.

Substantial discounts on bulk quantities of Jossey-Bass books are available to corporations, professional associations, and other organizations. For details and discount information, contact the special sales department at Jossey-Bass.

Manufactured in the United States of America.

Library of Congress Cataloging-in-Publication Data

Wheeler, Steven
Channel champions : how leading companies build new strategies to serve customers / Steven Wheeler, Evan Hirsh ; foreword by William F. Stasior.
p.  cm. — (The Jossey-Bass business & management series)  (A Strategy & business book)
Includes bibliographical references and index.
ISBN 0-7879-5034-3
1. Marketing.   2. Marketing—Management.   I. Hirsh, Evan II. Title.   III. Series.   IV. Series: A Strategy & business book.
HF5415.W484   1999
658.8—dc21            99-37791

FIRST EDITION
*HB Printing*  10 9 8 7 6 5 4 3 2 1

The Jossey-Bass
Business & Management Series

To my inspirations: Warren, Marilyn, Marisa, Evan, and Melanie
—Steven Wheeler

To my parents, Esta and Jack,
for their tremendous love and support
—Evan Hirsh

We want to acknowledge Stuart Crainer
for his help in shaping the manuscript and our ideas
and for his expert editorial assistance.

# Contents

# Foreword

For most of this century, Booz·Allen & Hamilton has been working with the world's largest companies and the teams that lead them. Although this period of history has been as furious as it has been fruitful, the topics that now occupy the busy calendars of CEOs and their leadership groups have not changed much from two or more decades ago. Today, as in the past, business leaders are concerned with how to make their companies more competitive while keeping costs in line and managing assets. Business leaders today, as in the past, want to create shareholder value, gain market share, and extend their company's capabilities and reach. While the issues confronting today's leaders are the same as in the past, the context in which those issues must be addressed has changed.

Today's business context is more complex than the environment of the past. That is not to say that previous eras were easier than this one. Success in the past—just as now—has never been easy to achieve. But unlike before, businesses today are confronted with a higher level of complexity brought about by globalization, new technologies, rapidly shifting conditions in the marketplace, and competition arising from the most unexpected places. Entire industries—the minicomputer industry, for example—have come into being, reached their apex, and fallen into the abyss of decline in little more than a decade. Others, like the computer mainframe business, which was once almost written off, have come roaring back.

In some industries, focusing on a company's core capabilities and primary business interest is the route to renewed vigor and prolonged health. Other businesses require the ability to be continuously innovative. Some companies, to prosper and grow, have had to reinvent themselves completely. Monsanto, for example, shed itself of its decades-old chemical business to become a bioengineering concern, while Westinghouse, one of America's oldest companies, transformed itself from a company known mostly for its power-generating equipment, including nuclear powerplants, into a media company that renamed itself CBS.

To survive and prosper, some companies have formed linkages with their chief rivals while others have severed linkages with their closest friends. Seen one way, this has been a period of mergers, alliances, and outright acquisitions. Seen another, it has been a period of divestitures, uncouplings, and recouplings. Seen all ways, it has been an era of complexity.

Today's perennial problems, unlike yesterday's, require a host of new, highly individualized solutions. Since the level of complexity is so high, the ability to create cookie-cutter solutions is at an all-time low. As a result, what matters is the ability to analyze problems carefully, quickly, and creatively. What matters is solving problems in fresh and disciplined ways. What matters is the ability to think about a subject while keeping the market in mind. What matters most is creativity.

The aim of *Strategy & Business* books is not to tell business leaders what to think. That would be both presumptuous—even foolhardy—given the rapid rate of change, the diversity of companies' situations, and the personalities of today's business leaders. Rather, the aim is to tell business leaders what to think *about.* The difference between *what to think* and *what to think about* is the difference between a rigid list of thoughts dictated by some font of wisdom, and an agenda set out for discussion. In the current period, the ability to discuss, reason, and argue scenarios and points-of-view beats rigid dictation every time.

Over the last several years, Booz·Allen has spent a lot of time mulling over the corporate agenda. It has done so by interviewing leaders, surveying firms, reviewing its own assignments, and consulting with academics. The contents of this book series—and this book on *Channel Champions*—reflect the contents of the business agenda.

What we have found in our research is that the big concerns over defining values and vision, managing people and risk, adapting to changed markets and new technology, and assessing channels and portfolio mix have only become more important as competition intensifies, the speed of computers multiplies, companies become more complex, and the economy becomes increasingly global.

At the same time, because of external pressures and changing management approaches, new ways of thinking about those concerns have swept through boardrooms and across factory floors with remarkable synchronicity. Some of these shifts reflect radically different orientations; others are wholly pragmatic in nature.

In our own work, we have recently seen the focus of the CEO agenda shift toward growing the top line rather than cutting costs and toward managing the new corporation instead of restructuring the old one. As we see it, three variations on these themes reflect the new agenda for CEOs and their top teams:

Managing for growth

Business process redesign, the next generation

The new organization

It seems clear what has caused CEOs to shift their focus. Many major companies, though not all, have completed the first wave of business process reengineering (BPR) and have thus achieved the first 80 percent or so of cost restructuring. They must now look to revenue growth for the next quantum leap in performance improvement. This situation puts managers in an expansive frame of mind that the rebound in corporate profits over the past several years undoubtedly reinforces.

At the same time, the wave of delayering, restructuring, and reengineering has left many companies in a twilight world between the old and the new. Traditional management processes have been discarded and dismantled; new ones are not always comfortably in place. Learning to manage in the post-restructured world has become a life-and-death priority, which has implications for the CEO's role in shaping a company's core capabilities and critical priorities and in determining which functions to outsource and which to leave in-house.

- *Emerging markets.* Even with Asia's current economic problems, most CEOs look to the emerging markets there and in Latin America (and to a much lesser and potentially myopic extent, eastern Europe) as the keys to future growth. On the one hand, there is the infrastructure boom ($1 trillion by 2000, according to some estimates); on the other, there is an almost infinite potential consumer market as more and more segments of these huge populations enter the market economy. Already, there are about 300 million "consumers" who have purchase power parity in the world's emerging markets. And that number represents only 10 percent or so of the total population of those areas.
- *New products, channels, and services.* The ability to sustain innovation in products, channels, and services is becoming a principal source of competitive advantage across a broad range of industries.
- *Acquisitions, mergers, alliances, and post-merger integration.* As balance sheets have improved, the number of corporate acquisitions has started to rebound dramatically. In fact, there is even evidence that part of the value liberated by recent acquisitions is being captured by the acquirer's shareholders and not just by those of the acquiree, which has overwhelmingly been the outcome historically. This trend is consistent with our observation that today's acquisitions appear to have a greater fit with the acquirers' core strategies and capabilities than was true in the past.
- *Strengthened "blocking and tackling."* Our clients are placing increased emphasis on the basics in their businesses: enhanced customer care; better marketing and sales force management; and improved, tactical pricing. Much of this change is overdue. Despite the claims of many analysts of BPR, recent rounds of reengineering and restructuring have left many of these basic processes weaker than before.

Relative emphasis among these growth routes necessarily varies. Our own analysis of one hundred companies with an above-average increase in shareholder wealth over the past two decades suggests that expansion in emerging markets is the greatest source of growth; breakout strategies that redefine the basis of competition in mature industries come second; and continuous product innovation and brand building come third. Acquisitions worked less well, with a few notable exceptions.

To capture differentiated growth, CEOs need to foster new and enhanced competencies and attitudes within their organizations. Innovation, for example, has long been viewed as being as much the product of lucky breaks as of a business capability that one can design, upgrade, and manage. As a result, many organizations avoid managing their innovation capability for fear of tampering with creative forces that they do not wholly understand. In fact, as companies such as the Chrysler Corporation and the Sony Corporation have shown, companies can design and manage innovation capability in a number of ways. These include strengthening the business processes associated with understanding markets, planning product lines, managing technology, and developing products or processes; improving measurement systems that track innovation; and developing systematic processes to capture and deploy organizational learning and best practices.

Similarly, to capture the full long-term potential of emerging markets, CEOs will have to move the center of gravity of their organizations, their managerial brain trusts, and their own mind-sets toward these markets—and there is a long way to go. Winning in emerging markets also requires a different type of decision-making process. The pace of change is so fast that traditional planning processes simply do not work. For example, markets that took a decade to develop in the United States and six years in Japan are evolving in less than two years in some parts of China.

What is needed is strategic entrepreneurship, a relatively clear view of long-term objectives, and a strong set of strategic boundaries that can be used to screen opportunities. CEOs also require a highly entrepreneurial approach to creating and exploiting opportunities and shifting between scenarios as they unfold.

Growth also brings uncertainty and more complexity, however, which has implications for how companies must think about risk management. Among the "perennials" on the CEO agenda, we have found that risk management is the issue demanding the most attention.

As CEOs think about growth, their time frames are lengthening. We love to ask clients to estimate their time horizon. Answers vary, depending on the near-term health of their businesses, but strategic focus has moved out to about seven years. On earlier occasions, eighteen months was not unusual. During the last couple of years, our firm has experienced a surge of engagements focused on modeling the relatively distant future and on leading management teams through strategic simulations or sophisticated war games for their industries.

Changing demographics, technology advances, and global shifts have far-reaching implications for competitive boundaries and patterns of demand in virtually every industry. CEOs increasingly view one of their core roles as stimulating their companies' perspectives on what the future will bring. The boldest among them will select a scenario and remold their businesses accordingly.

CEOs have long understood their role in building the corporate vision. Today, this focus is being complemented by a drive to establish and entrench clear corporate values. These are not simply a means to edify the spirit but are vehicles to communicate strategic focus and operating boundaries to all employees. This represents a shift from the focus of most strategists ten years ago.

The breakthrough implies a focus on both vision and communication. The entire organization must understand the company's strategic direction and feel empowered to reach that goal.

A related trend in organizations is renewed interest in the role of the corporate center or core. At a recent symposium at which Booz·Allen partners discussed the most important business issues on the agendas of the firm's clients, we discovered that a majority of the participating partners were working with major companies to retune and redefine the role of the corporate center.

To some degree, that reassessment relates to the need to change management processes to fit the post-restructured corporation. It is also driven by external, competitive pressures, however; the same market pressures that compelled companies to lower costs are forcing them to rethink the integrative logic of their business portfolios.

Much of the thinking in this field comes back to address which businesses belong in the corporate portfolio and how the parent can add value rather than subtract it, as is too frequently the case. In addition to the traditional debate over the most appropriate forms of strategic and financial performance systems, this wave of reexamination is focused on building truly global organizations (in many cases, with traditional "center" functions being distributed geographically), on conceiving and managing strategic alliances and other extended enterprise relationships, and on some of the "softer" forms of added value.

The latter include the inculcation of shared corporate values and identity and the capture and deployment of organizational learning and best practices. Increasingly, corporate added value is more a matter of applying intellectual capital than of sponsoring scale economies in unit costs.

We are also seeing greater top-level attention focused on managing through processes. The wave of restructuring, reengineering, and delayering demands different management approaches than those used in the past. Yet the new approaches have been slow to develop. In a recent analysis that we conducted of twenty-eight "post-reengineered" companies, we found that in most cases, the CEOs and their top management teams were continuing to manage essentially as before. They used the same decision, planning, and control processes and the same management information and reporting systems. Most recognized the disconnection but were uncertain about how to resolve it. The answer lies in taking the following actions:

- Reorienting top executives to manage and enable "processes" rather than organization units
- Explicit reengineering of the decision-making processes involving top management itself, with related changes in authority delegation and style
- Creating new performance management systems that complement the reengineered world and incorporate an ability to learn

In beginning to address these issues, CEOs are also beginning to take more seriously some of the concepts that they nominally embraced over the past several years. The horizontal organization, team-based management, the learning organization, empowerment, and similar concepts have had their place in the executive lexicon for several years. The body language of most CEOs continued to reinforce older, more hierarchical traditions, however. This is now beginning to change as CEOs gain a greater understanding of these ideas and become more sincere in their desire to practice them.

The final element of the new organization relates to the players themselves. Building the management team is always a CEO agenda item. Today, virtually all CEOs with whom we talk say that creating greater entrepreneurship and teamwork among their top one hundred managers is their Number 1 challenge.

There are several drivers behind this renewed focus on the top team. Above all, the pace and volume of change that most corporations face demand that the load be shared; the CEO cannot typically expect to shoulder it alone. Then, too, there is a need to rebuild the social contract between managers and the company. One consequence of restructuring and downsizing has been a unilateral revocation of implied loyalties.

CEOs are exploring various approaches to reengineering their teams, including explicit team-building exercises, adjustments to measurement and rewards systems, and experimentation with such devices as internal "venture funds" designed to stimulate entrepreneurship. We are also seeing a renewed focus on selection, including a willingness to reach outside the home team to enlist the best athletes.

As CEO agendas evolve, the natural question is whether the current focus is correct. In our view, the new agenda is properly directed. Nevertheless, it is almost certain that the next decade will see a sorting of winners from losers at least as significant as the one that occurred during the last two decades. Fewer than half of the Fortune 500 listed twenty years ago are still on the list today, and a fair number of the survivors owe their position to their leviathan scale rather than to stellar performance.

Companies that lost their position failed because they had insufficient insight into their customers' needs and the implications of technology and new channels. In addition, they allowed service bottlenecks and excess costs to accumulate in their delivery systems. As a result, overseas and greenfield competitors were able to outdeliver and undercut them.

In theory, the new CEO agenda will help business leaders avoid similar missteps in the future. It will do this in a number of ways: the concentration on growth and innovation implies improved customer understanding and strengthened value propositions; the second wave of BPR will improve value while keeping costs lean; and the new organization will focus on shared learning, continual improvement, and greater entrepreneurship. Overall, we observe a more concerted attempt by CEOs to understand and position their companies for the future.

In practice, of course, some companies and some CEOs will do better than others. That is the nature of competition. From our vantage point, though, it is clear that the winners will be those CEOs who can integrate the new agenda with their own clear vision while simplifying the execution challenge and inspiring their organizations to perform beyond all expectations.

*New York, New York*  
*July 1999*

William F. Stasior  
Chairman and Chief Executive  
Booz·Allen & Hamilton

# Preface

A single brilliant insight can create a business empire. Ask Michael Dell. His $12 billion inspiration was that he could bypass the dealer channel through which personal computers were then being sold. Instead, he would sell directly to customers and build products to order. Dell created a new channel for selling and manufacturing PCs.

The new channel meant that the company wasn't hostage to the mark-ups of resellers. Nor was it burdened with large inventories. In fact, it was the ultimate in virtuous circles. Costs were low and profits high. "You actually get to have a relationship with the customer," explains Dell. "And that creates valuable information, which in turn allows us to leverage our relationships with both suppliers and customers. Couple that information with technology and you have the infrastructure to revolutionize the fundamental business models of major global companies."[1]

Today, other companies are following Michael Dell's example by discovering new and different channels to market. In many cases, it is their ability to invent and manage these channels that is revolutionizing the industries they are in. What a growing number of the world's leading companies are realizing is that channel management has the power to change the rules of the game.

The aim of this book is to stimulate your thinking on the relative importance of channel issues. It doesn't try to be a how-to book or a

cure-all for every known corporate problem. Instead, it describes best practice in the field of channel management and gives you specific, real-world
examples of how companies in industries from floor coverings to high
technology have used channels to secure competitive advantage and add
value to their business performance. It also outlines a systematic process
for making channels work for you—not the day-to-day details, which will
differ for each industry and each corporate culture, but an overview of five
stages that can be observed in every successful channel implementation.

## What Is Channel Management?

Channel management is more than distribution or logistics—though
these are obviously important. It is a way of thinking, a way of making
new connections with customers to exploit new commercial opportunities. A channel is the essence of the way customers and a business
interact—everything about how and where people purchase a product
or service and how and where they use that product or service. It is a
business's route to its customers and a business's ongoing relationship
with its customers. It determines the entire buying and owning (or con-
suming) experience. When you think in terms of channels you should
be thinking strategy: effective channel management offers the chance
to reinvent not just your business but the industry you're in.

Take a simple example like canned goods. Some customers will always prefer the traditional channel, visiting their local grocery store or
supermarket to buy fruit salad, beans, or whatever. Some customers on
some occasions will purchase the same product at a convenience store.
But others will welcome the introduction of a home shopping service,
via telephone, cable service, or the Internet. In all instances, the product—
the canned food—is the same; only the channels change. But it is the
channel that imbues the relationship with additional value.

At present, much the same applies to Amazon.com, the upstart that
has become the biggest book retailer in the world simply by offering
book buyers a new channel—via the Internet. The product is still a traditional book—only the channel has altered. Instead of simply buying a
book, consumers select a purchase and a reading experience that varies
greatly depending on the channel chosen. At the newer stores of Borders
and Barnes & Noble, where coffee bars and musical entertainment

accompany book buying, the channel experience is quite different from either a traditional bookstore or Amazon.com.

Channel management, therefore, is a systematic means of reaching and taking care of your customers wherever they are and however they like to be reached. It is about identifying the most important customers to your business. It is how you consummate the relationship with customers. It is how you communicate with customers. It is how you create and capture value from the product after the initial sale.

The end result of effective channel management is good for your business—no matter what your business may be. Effective channel management enhances customer service. It offers wider choice for consumers. It creates innovative responses to their needs and aspirations. It may change the fundamental definition of the business you are in.

# Contents

Section One establishes the basic premise. In Chapter One, we cover the reasons why managing channels effectively is vital to corporate success. The traditional source of competitive value—product-based differentiation—is diminishing in importance in the global economy, where any physical thing can be copied adequately somewhere and any manufacturer can reach any potential customer anywhere in the world. The differences that can't be copied easily are differences in service and support—in relationship with the customer—and those differences are all features of the channel. Chapter Two develops the idea of service excellence. It shows how an effective channel works both ways, bringing the company information that allows it to adapt to the real needs of the marketplace quickly and efficiently while keeping customers too happy to look elsewhere for the goods they want.

Section Two presents the five essential steps for channel management, devoting a chapter to each. The steps form a continuous cycle: understand the buying and ownership needs of your customers, develop new channel concepts for each segment of your customer base, pilot test to polish the economics and competitive positioning of the channel concepts, roll out the concepts rapidly once they're developed, and study the results and refine your position—thereby improving your understanding of your customers and beginning the cycle again.

Section Three takes a step back to look at the whole channel management process and deal with potential pitfalls and opportunities. One of the key elements of channel management is developing enough separate channels to address each recognizable segment of the market—but the more channels you have, the greater the chance that they will interfere with one another. Chapter Eight discusses ways to recognize potential channel conflict and head it off before it can pose a problem. Chapter Nine turns to the need to stay ahead of the game, constantly developing and refining channels and staying alert for new ways to support customers and keep them tied to the company. A company that relies on one tried-and-true set of operations is apt to wake up and find that someone else has reinvented it out of business. In the end, success is a matter of one—one customer makes the decision to buy and stay with the company, and that one decision repeated over and over is what keeps you in business. Chapter Ten looks ahead to the interconnected world of electronic commerce, where companies can work effectively with their customers in segments of one, producing exactly what the customer wants at exactly the right time, maximizing satisfaction while minimizing costs and maintaining a channel that will resist the inroads of would-be competitors.

None of this is airy, pie-in-the-sky forecasting. In industry after industry, companies are finding *right now* that effective channel management is simple good business. Throughout the book, you'll find examples of the current best practice—companies we call "channel champions"—drawn from our experience as management consultants and from research in North America, Europe, South America, and Asia. The result is not another prescription for success but an introduction to a flexible and powerful means of viewing the emerging corporate world and prospering within it. Our intention throughout has been to provoke debate and prompt executives to examine the potential of channel management in their own organizations. We can't all be Michael Dell—but we can all learn important lessons from Dell's success.

*July 1999*

Steven Wheeler
*Munich, Germany*

Evan Hirsh
*Chicago, Illinois*

# Channel Champions

# Section One

# (Re)think Channels

Product-based differentiation has traditionally been the cornerstone of corporate competitiveness. Better products led to market dominance. While this was once true, however, it is no longer the case. Instead, better service is becoming a key factor.

1.  *Three factors explain the declining impact of pure product-based differentiation:*

- Increasing global competition makes it harder to control any market.
- Rapid technological evolution has shortened product life cycles.
- Products are more quickly emulated, copied, matched, or outdone, no matter where they are produced and no matter by whom.

But differentiating yourself from the competition remains important. Now, in addition to product differentiation, companies are differentiating themselves through the services they offer to their customers. The services consist not only of the nonproduct offerings (financing, delivery, warranties) but also the entire set of purchase and after-sales support interactions. In other words, the experiences and relationships that are delivered by the channel are what actually constitute it.

Managing these channels has, as a result, become highly important and is already being used by some top-performing companies, channel champions.

2.   *As product differentiation declines, service differentiation is becoming ever more important.*

Service excellence is not bland or ethereal. It is concerned with delivering substantive and measurable benefits to customers—benefits that customers value and are willing to pay for. In delivering such benefits, channels fulfill three roles:

- Information flow (inward and outward)
- Logistics to deliver products and services to the end consumer
- Value-added services that augment the product or service

Channel management offers the opportunity to deliver new combinations of product and services. In today's business world, it is the product and service bundle that provides differentiation and competitive advantage.

# Chapter 1
# The Channel Advantage
## From Products to Customer Relationships

> We must develop systems and support structures, as well as
> products, that establish competitive advantages for our dealers and
> allow them to compete on more than just product and price on a
> transactional basis.
>     —James Hebe, president and CEO,
>         Freightliner Corporation[1]

In the beginning there was the product.

Centuries ago, craftsmen labored over their products. Such was their
devotion that they literally crafted each piece, inch by inch, to create
things of usefulness or beauty, or both. And in the industrial age,
whether you were a manufacturer like General Motors or a movie stu-
dio like Warner Brothers, products were the basic unit of competitive
strength and weakness.

Though the new companies made more products more efficiently
than the old craftsmen ever imagined possible, the fundamental premise
was the same: better or cheaper products attracted more customers;
more satisfied customers led to repeat sales and, in turn, to increased
profits. Tangible attributes—the touch, appearance, taste, and smell of
the product—were all. Products were the simple benchmark by which
every business was measured. QED.

Clearly, this is a simplified interpretation of past preoccupations. But it is (with a few glorious exceptions) generally true. Indeed, even now, most manufacturers think primarily of the product when going to market. They think of the most efficient way of making the product. They think of its attributes. They look at it. They touch it. They taste it. They consider how it should be priced. They think of how customers and groups of customers interact with the product. Success or failure is seen as being product-related. Get the product right and everything else will fall effortlessly into place.

It is a well-established corporate habit, but focusing only on the product is a dangerous game. Henry Ford may have invented mass production and all but invented a mass market for the car, but his blind faith in the Model T nearly pushed his company to self-destruction.

Henry Ford is long gone and Ford is now refocusing on brands and channels, but his preoccupations live on with other vehicle manufacturers. Products *uber alles.* One element of the turbulent McDonald's story of recent years has been a continued focus on the product. Ideas such as the Arch Deluxe and the 55-cent Big Mac have largely backfired on the company's U.S. operations. There is more to McDonald's than its product—as demonstrated by the growth of its Special Points of Distribution (SPODs) in airports and shopping malls, its venture into Mexican food retailing, and the growth of the Playlands. However, with the support of the franchisees holding ownership in the old channel format, product-dominated marketing campaigns remain the company's major focus.[2]

Product differentiation can easily become product fascination. History is littered with brilliantly innovative products that few people bought and that are now stacked gathering dust in warehouses. One of the classic examples is the Sony Betamax video system. This was a great idea. It was a truly excellent product made by a consistently innovative and imaginative company. Yet the only place to find a Betamax video now is in a museum.

The global standard is VHS, which was originated by Matsushita. While Matsushita developed VHS video and licensed the technology, Sony developed the immeasurably better Betamax but failed to license the technology. It assumed its product would be persuasive, but being better was not good enough for Betamax.

Now, Sony sells through multiple channels, including its company stores in major metro markets. Simple product-based differentiation rapidly diminished.

But even if you get it right, in the twilight of the twentieth century product-based differentiation is becoming harder to sustain. Product superiority is usually a fleeting illusion. Indeed, the confident commercial assertion of QED is rapidly giving way to a more doom-laden prognosis: pure product differentiation, RIP.

## Copying the Advantage

The decreasing importance of product-based differentiation as the primary source of competitive advantage can be attributed to two main factors:

First, there is the globalization of competition. No matter what business you are in, life is becoming more competitive. You are faced with having to keep abreast of product developments on a global scale. No matter what your resources, this is virtually impossible. Geographical and physical divides have disappeared. There are fewer barriers to the flow of information. If you improve a product in Beijing, thanks to technology, someone in Baltimore will soon be able to find out how you did it—or vice versa. (It is notable that in this new world order, the threat and the opportunity are inextricably linked. Global accessibility is both the opportunity and the source of potential competition.)

The second factor in the decline in importance of product-based differentiation is rapid technology evolution. Technological change means that products require continual enhancement just to survive. Product life cycles are perpetually shortening.

These two factors give rise to the inevitable result of rapid imitation of new products and product enhancements. Camera models, for example, have a life span as short as six months. The number of models on the market has continued to grow as competitors avidly copy each other's innovations. This desperate race with no end makes it clear that products still matter. Of course they do. But having auto-focus or the latest gimmick is the price of entry rather than the winning ticket.

The daunting truth is that copying products has never been easier. Any company that finds a way to protect patents and copyrights is among the surest bets to become a booming business in the new millennium. Goods that are close substitutes for each other in the customers' eyes are more generally available than ever before. And we are not talking about street vendors in Malaysia selling pond water masquerading as Chanel or bootleggers in Beijing selling Michael Jackson CDs produced in a backyard. Virtually any product on earth can be speedily replicated.

Products that rely on tangible attributes are particularly susceptible to imitation. A Burmese Black & Decker copy will, in all likelihood, look the same and do the job in the same way. But it will probably not look the same for very long or be able to do the job for much longer than the time it takes you to leave the country. Street peddlers of watches have followed this strategy for many years. If they say it is a genuine Swiss watch and it looks and feels like a genuine Swiss watch, you may well be convinced. The product is persuasive because it appears to do the job, even if you know the after-sales service is nonexistent.[3]

It would be easy to assume that product copying is the preserve of the desperate, opportunistic, or poor. This is not the case. The world's great corporations are engaged in a constant round of me-too developments. Take a look around.

In financial services, any new product—whether it be an account for the elderly or a more flexible mortgage—is copied almost instantly. Products and services emerge in a constant stream as old ones are tinkered with, replaced, or revamped, and entirely new ones introduced. In one year the U.K.-based bank, NatWest, introduced 240 new products or improvements to existing products.

There is no longer anything particularly unusual in this. Explaining his company's strategy, George Schaefer, chief executive of the Cincinnati-based Fifth Third Bank, says: "Hustle. That's us. It's what we do. In financial services, where if anyone in town comes out with a new product everyone else has it five seconds later, what really matters is daily execution."[4] (Schaefer gets to the nub of the argument: change products all you like, but how and where you deliver them on a daily basis is the real battlefield.)

In industry after industry, today's bright ideas quickly become permanent fixtures. Today's leading edge is tomorrow's condition of entry. In the car market, anti-lock brakes were heralded as a major step forward. BMW trumpeted its invention. Now, anti-lock brakes are no longer an advantage, and BMW has moved onto "telematics" in a joint venture with Motorola.[5]

Look at shampoos. P&G labored long and hard in developing two-in-one shampoo. After more than a decade spent perfecting the technology, it launched the product with the usual fanfare. Within two years, most of its competitors had followed suit. Years of investment and a mold-breaking product had provided only a fleeting advantage.[6]

So products *can* provide you with a competitive advantage. But it is not sustainable for very long—and this period is becoming ever shorter in duration.

This phenomenon is typical of maturing markets and is increasingly common across industries. Nowhere is it more evident than in the personal computer industry. Over two generations, product-based and even performance-based differentiation has dramatically declined.[7]

## Repercussions for Suppliers

Declining product differentiation has implications on how, where, and why people buy products. Fundamental assumptions about the supplier-customer relationship are overturned and there are sizable ripples elsewhere. With product dominance reduced, the balance of power in relationships dramatically shifts. Control of the channel rather than control of the product becomes paramount.

For example, think of what happens to suppliers. As product-based differentiation declines, the traditional sources of suppliers' power are weakened. This has three important repercussions:

First, and most obviously, having a more advanced or more effective product no longer guarantees success. The Apple Mac may still be lauded as a groundbreaking product, but it wasn't enough to sustain Apple. Of course, companies always want to have a better product—look at the attempts by Burger King to try and displace McDonald's as the french-fries leader or Colgate's huge ($100 million) onslaught on Crest.

The second area in which the power of suppliers is weakened is brand pull. Customers are more fickle than ever before. They won't automatically come running when they hear a supplier's name. Fever-pitch competition in brands means no one is safe—a point demonstrated by the drama of Marlboro Friday, Diaper Tuesday, and the Soap Wars in Europe between Unilever and P&G.[8] Even brand giants can no longer automatically call the tune.

The third area of developing weakness is that having a large established customer base no longer guarantees future success. As an example, look at how Coke (with Sprite) and Pepsi (with Storm) struck into the lemon-lime category. It was a profitable and stable market, long dominated by 7-Up. But it was differentiated from colas and other flavors so that the big players saw it as attractive and entered. The message is that no business is sacrosanct. No business can afford to feel comfortable.

The parameters of a business (any business) can change overnight. An apparently secure customer base is an invitation to competitors, not a measure of security. And, to really turn things on their head, companies can actually receive plaudits when they announce that they want to reduce the number of customers they have.

The reality is that power has flowed downstream from the producers to the channels in industry after industry. "Category killer" retail formats, like Wal-Mart, The Home Depot, Best Buy, Car Max, Borders, Tire America, Office Max—the list goes on and on—put pressure on suppliers for low costs and high service levels. Traditional sources of power—good products, the pull of a brand, an installed customer base, a broad product line—have diminished in their impact. Added momentum has come from technical advances—everything from bar coding to 800 numbers—that have increased channels' ability to improve service levels and lower costs, thereby increasing their value to customers and their power over suppliers (as Exhibit 1.1 demonstrates). Such trends will surely accelerate.

**Exhibit 1.1  Technology as an Enabler to the Downstream Flow of Power**

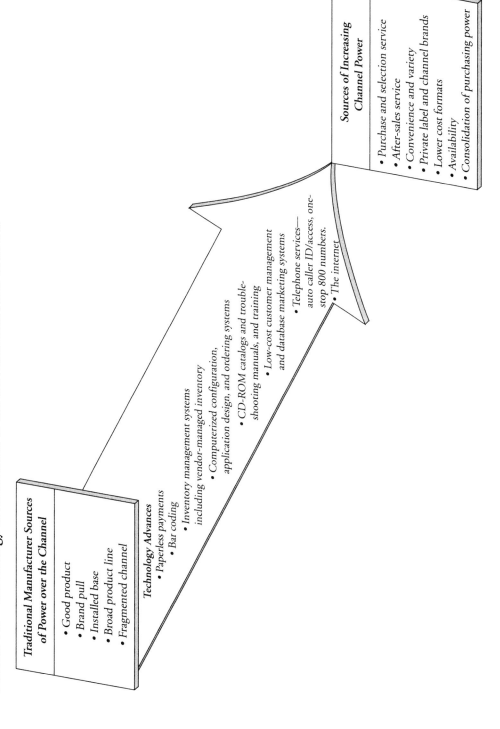

*Traditional Manufacturer Sources of Power over the Channel*

- Good product
- Brand pull
- Installed base
- Broad product line
- Fragmented channel

*Technology Advances*

- Paperless payments
- Bar coding
- Inventory management systems including vendor-managed inventory
- Computerized configuration, application design, and ordering systems
- CD-ROM catalogs and trouble-shooting manuals, and training
- Low-cost customer management and database marketing systems
- Telephone services—auto caller ID/access, one-stop 800 numbers.
- The internet

*Sources of Increasing Channel Power*

- Purchase and selection service
- After-sales service
- Convenience and variety
- Private label and channel brands
- Lower cost formats
- Availability
- Consolidation of purchasing power

# Differentiation Through Services

So how can we break this spiral? If product differentiation is becoming less and less important, what else is there? What lies beyond? As is so often the case, the solution lies within the problem. While product-based differentiation is declining in power, it should not be concluded that differentiation is unimportant. Indeed, differentiation remains the fundamental route to competitive advantage. But the question now is, *Differentiation of what?*

The answer is increasingly that differentiation is achieved as much through the services surrounding the product as through the product itself.

As a result, manufacturers are increasingly turning their attention to the value added—or dissipated—beyond the factory gate. Little wonder. This value can often be as high as 25 percent to 35 percent for many products. (See Exhibit 1.2.) Indeed, 90 percent of the profit potential from the life cycle of a mass market car is not concerned with the first sale of the product.

So in addition to product differentiation we have service differentiation. This is based on segmenting customers according to how they want to purchase and interact with the product. The source of differentiation then becomes a combination—or bundle—of products and services. In this model, the channel becomes vital.

Just as products are manufactured on a production line, product–service bundles are delivered by a channel. The channel must add value to the customer. (Remember W. Edwards Deming's observation, "The consumer is the most important part of the production line." The same point applies to channel management.)

*A channel can be defined as how and where you purchase a product (or service) and how and where you use the product. It is the essence of how customers and the product interact. It is a supplier's route to the customer and ongoing relationship with the customer.*

Good channel management has, as a result, become much more than just a basic necessity of doing business: it now has the potential to differentiate one manufacturer from another. Channels, and the bundle

**Exhibit 1.2    The Value Added Beyond the Factory Gate**

*Automobiles*

| |
|---|
| Dealer Gross Margin 14% |
| Logistics 4% |
| Operating Income 5% |
| SG&A 11% |
| Manufacturing Value Added 20% |
| Materials and Inbound Freight 46% |

*Building Products*
*Vinyl Siding*

| |
|---|
| Distributor Gross Margin 30% |
| Operating Income 10% |
| SG&A 11% |
| Manufacturing Value Added 12% |
| Materials and Inbound Freight 41% |

*Electrical Products*
*Power Conditioners and Transformers*

| |
|---|
| Distributor Gross Margin 21% |
| Operating Income 8% |
| SG&A 16% |
| Manufacturing Value Added 23% |
| Materials and Inbound Freight 32% |

*Automotive Aftermarket Products*
*Tires*

| |
|---|
| Distributor Gross Margin 25% |
| Operating Income 5% |
| SG&A 32% |
| Manufacturing Value Added 20% |
| Materials and Inbound Freight 32% |

☐ *Primarily After-Plant Channel Costs*

*Note: Excludes costs of non-warranty parts and service*

of services they bring with them, are a crucial differentiating force. As a result, how a company manages its channels is a critical lever in improving business performance. This is what a growing number of successful companies are realizing. We call them "channel champions," and they are leading the way.

# Introducing the Channel Champions

The range of companies benefiting from effective channel management, as well as the wide-ranging nature of their businesses, makes it clear that channels are a fact of business life across all sectors and industries. Channel management is as relevant to a car manufacturer as to a retail chain, as important to a bank as to a dishwasher maker.

Look at what has happened at Levi Strauss. The product has remained much the same over the decades. What has changed is how the company manages and perceives the channels through which it sells its products. "We are appealing to a broad range of consumers for different wearing occasions in casual wear, and as long as they feel that our products fulfill their psychological needs as well as the product requirements, we've made our mark," says CEO Robert Haas. In a paragraph, Haas pithily redefines his business for the new millennium. The channel—the psychological experience—is the thing; the physical satisfaction of the product still matters, but it's secondary. "We are in the comfort business and I don't just mean physical comfort. I mean we are providing psychological comfort—the feeling of security that, when you enter a room of strangers or even work colleagues, you are attired within the band of acceptability. Although obviously what a consumer defines as psychological comfort may vary from sub-segment to sub-segment," says Haas.[9] The new challenge lies in learning about the psychology of your real and potential customers, identifying segment after segment. (This does not guarantee success if your product is increasingly out of step with the marketplace—something Levi Strauss discovered to its eventual cost.)

No matter whether you run a pet food store, make tires, or sell used cars, improving existing channels and opening up new channels through which customers can interact with your product is perhaps the most potent means of bringing your business to life.

Channel management issues manifest themselves in a variety of ways:

- Deteriorating relationships with the channel
- Declining share, inability to grow
- Increasing costs through the channel, but no increase in services provided
- Major distributors or retailers expand, consolidate, or add new product lines
- Decreasing relative margins
- Declining end customer satisfaction

- Competitors finding superior ways to provide goods and services to the market
- Pricing exceptions proliferate
- Major shift in share of a particular channel

Increasingly, we hear top executives refer to channel management as one of their top concerns:

- "I'm not sure I have the right channel."
   Need different distributors or retailers
   Need to sell direct
- "My dealers (or distributors) aren't performing."
   They aren't growing
   Their costs are too high
   Service levels are flat or declining
   They don't respond
- "I have conflicts between my different channels."
- "I can't reach new market segments."
- "I can't realize all the benefits of my internal reengineering efforts without making changes in the channels."

The need for channel management crosses all divides. Think of a museum. If there is a museum in your town, you will probably pay it a visit at some time. You will then consider that the matter is closed. You have assuaged your civic interest. Part of the job of the museum, however, should be to give people repeated opportunities to interact with it, if only to maintain and increase its membership and attendance levels. It could do so in a myriad of ways—inviting school visits, changing exhibitions, involving people in archaeological digs, allowing people behind the scenes, taking exhibits on the road, creating educational puzzles and games. Greater interaction gives people the opportunity to become more and more involved. Providing a variety of ways to experience the same product keeps it fresh—and there are many ways of retaining freshness.

The logic is inexorable. Across many industries advancing levels of competition are resulting in increased power for channels. One thing leads to another. There is, as we have discussed, greater availability of close substitutes on basic product values. Competing products can do the job, look the part, and even (outside the back-street ripoffs) stand up to the wear and tear of daily use. Manufacturer-driven values are no longer a sure route to competitive strength. The reality is that quality levels in product manufacturing have improved. At the same time, companies are experiencing more difficulty in innovating distinctive new products, driven by diminishing product life cycles and faster competitor responses to new product developments.

This leads to more customer choice and attempts to address the needs of more focused customer segments—indeed, segments of one. This demands ever more intimate knowledge of consumers, which increases the push toward nonproduct differentiation. It is no longer just the product that counts, but how, when, and where it is delivered to the customer.

Issues such as convenience, availability, purchase and ownership experiences, and after-sales service become increasingly important. This inevitably results in the differentiation and the power flowing downstream into the channels and to end customers.

As channels evolve to serve changing or finer customer demands, existing players lose ground or respond as new winners emerge. We have already mentioned Dell; think also of Gateway, which is now moving into selling computing rather than PCs. The company is not alone. A wave of channel champions is emerging across a broad range of industries:

• *Genuine Parts in the automotive aftermarket.* Genuine Parts helped transform the aftermarket auto parts wholesale distribution industry. Before its arrival, the industry was highly fragmented, with separate warehouse distributor and jobber structures. Genuine Parts, with sixty-three U.S. distribution centers supplying 5,200 "associate" jobbers, brings a large-scale, uniform, efficient warehouse operation to the business. It also offers sophisticated inventory management, an electronic interface with suppliers, jobbers, and installers, and extensive support for jobbers. The result? Significantly lower logistics costs, superior fill rates, reduced selling costs, increased purchasing leverage with suppliers, a wider product offering, a double-digit operating margin, and the expansion of automotive business sales from $1.5 billion in 1985 to $6 billion in 1997.

• *United Stationers in office supplies.* United Stationers grew from sales of $170 million in 1980 to $1.5 billion in 1992, acquiring a 50 percent share of the market. Now it has sales of $3 billion.

It virtually eliminated small, independent distributors (though it is now under pressure from low-cost, cash-and-carry office product warehouses). Its achievement was to totally restructure the office supply distribution industry. Prior to the company's taking action, it had an extremely fragmented distribution base. It introduced a well-managed product catalog and developed a distribution center network.

• *Lexus in automobiles.* Forget the impressive statistics—the Lexus took seven years, $2 billion, 1,400 engineers, 2,300 technicians, 450 prototypes, and generated 200 patents—and feel the service. Good car; fantastic, differentiating service.

• *AutoNation, Inc. (formerly known as Republic Industries) in transportation.* AutoNation is shaking up the car retailing industry, causing a wave of reactions from vehicle manufacturers. It owned 223 dealerships and had $13.5 billion in revenues in 1998. It is over four times larger than the next largest dealer group, VT Incorporated. In late 1996 and early 1997 it bought Alamo and National Car Rentals for $3.1 billion, and has bought and assimilated four other rental car companies including Value, Spirit, Snappy Rental (under the Car Temps USA name, competing with Enterprise), and EuroDollar. It has a chain of used car superstores, presently with more than thirty-five outlets (including the Driver's Mart acquisition in April 1998) and sales of around $1.4 billion, with plans to nearly double that number over the next two years. Since 1996, AutoNation has grown revenues at a rate of over 200 percent per year.

• *Saturn in automobiles.* With the launch of Saturn, GM realized that car buyers were fed up with the slick car salesmen and the poor service they found at many dealerships. Saturn created its own dealer network and, as result, increased repeat purchases and customer satisfaction dramatically. Rather than view the car narrowly as a product, the new approach recognized that customers wanted a bundle of transportation services. Saturn's brand development focused on the buying experience, service, and support. It was concerned with people and processes rather than the product. (Daewoo has gone one step further, cutting out the dealer network altogether. In effect, Daewoo is trying to do to autos what Dell has already done to PCs. It is experimenting in the United States and United Kingdom with highly nontraditional ways of selling vehicles.)

•   *The Home Depot in building products.* With twenty-seven quarters of consecutive record sales and record earnings, The Home Depot has seen its stock price increase at a compound annual rate of over 70 percent for the last eight years. Forty to fifty new stores are being added every year, as The Home Depot expands into new geographic markets such as the U.S. Northeast as well as California and Florida. Along the way, The Home Depot has revolutionized the do-it-yourself market with innovative channel management. Its annual sales now top $24 billion.

•   *W.W. Grainger in general industrial products.* Grainger provides one-stop convenience shopping for inhouse maintenance operations and general contractors. Its 332 branches with retail-style counter sales have a broad product offering backed by a widely distributed catalog (now available on CD-ROM) and extensive advertising. It boasts gross margins of 36 percent against the electrical wholesaler average of 27 percent. It is now making a major foray into electronic commerce.

•   *Wal-Mart in mass merchandising.* Wal-Mart recognized that many consumers want to buy affordably and get good service and name brands, so it forged partnerships with product companies like Procter & Gamble for direct purchase, stocking, and inventory management. The result: huge and profitable growth on the traditionally low-margin mass merchandise market.

•   *General Electric in appliances.* GE Appliances sells over 10 million appliances in 150 world markets, including refrigerators, freezers, ranges, cooktops, wall ovens, dishwashers, and washing machines. Its brands include the Monogram, GE Profile, Hotpoint, and RCA. Its achievement has been to keep one channel—the smaller, independent channel—alive and viable in the face of competition from Circuit City and the like, through offering superior logistics, after-sales service, and end-customer service.

- *Providian Bancorp in financial services.* Providian has built up a credit portfolio of more than $5 billion in only ten years, thanks to understanding its customers in ways never previously thought of and giving them exactly what they want. Providian can provide consumer credit on a one-to-one basis, so each customer has a personalized interest rate and set of repayment terms. Responsive yet proactive, Providian has reshaped financial services marketing and branding.

- *Snap-on Tools in tool supply.* For years Snap-on has bypassed the usual distribution channels to sell directly to its customers (garages and auto dealerships) via fleets of self-managed dealers on wheels. It sells high-quality tools at premium prices and cuts out the competition by going to where its customers work. It is now entering a new channel by supplying private label tools to Lowe's, a leading U.S. retailer.

# Chapter 2
# Channel Management
## A Framework for Revolution

In most manufacturing industries, distribution and product support remain underappreciated strategic assets. That situation will soon change because the global winners over the next ten to twenty years are going to be the companies with the best distribution organizations that also provide superb customer support. Engineering excellence, manufacturing efficiency, and quality are rapidly becoming givens; everyone is going to need them to be a player. Indeed, most companies deficient in those areas have already disappeared.

—DONALD V. FITES, CHAIRMAN AND CEO, CATERPILLAR[1]

Customer service is the heart of business and the heart of channel management.

Stating that service differentiation is increasingly vital should hardly be earth-shattering. However, turning it into a daily reality, a business strategy that actually happens, remains unusual. A great deal has been written about service since Tom Peters and Robert Waterman rediscovered it as a critical business issue in their 1982 best-seller, *In Search of Excellence.*

There continues to be a lot of vague talk about customer delight (Wow!) and the like. It is motivational and a lot can be learned from best practice, but the superficiality of Wow! is not—and never can be— a business strategy.

For all the books and seminars, service remains a misunderstood element of business. Often confused with teaching staff to smile and say "Have a nice day," it tends to sink in the mire of motherhood statements and touchy-feely approximations. We believe this is unnecessary. The same business rigor and professionalism once focused on the product can be brought to bear on service.

But this can only be achieved if the nature of service is understood. Very simply, good service is service that delivers what the customer wants when the customer wants it and at a price the customer is prepared to pay. As the deluge of publications and opinions testifies, this is not easy. Service is uniquely characterized by intangibility, the inseparability of production and consumption, variability, and perishability. Little wonder that it is elusive. In addition, customers are increasingly demanding. In their book *Up Against the Wal-Marts,* Don Taylor and Jeanne Smalling Archer conclude:

Customers want value
Customers like choices
Customers love anything new
Customers love long open-for-business hours
Customers love convenient locations
Customers want the convenience of one-stop shopping
Customers don't want hassles
Customers want a friendly, personal touch in a clean, fun place to shop.

This is no wish list. Companies must deliver.

In response, companies must create channels concerned with tangible value. It is not about attitude, nor superficial changes. It is about the customer primarily and about the channel secondarily. It is about the value that customers recognize, not on how much is created and transferred to the channel. A channel without customers is like a bath without water, but a lot more expensive. On-line grocery shopping, for example, is only worthwhile if people are prepared to pay for it. Not everyone will want to pay for someone else to pull their groceries off the shelf and deliver them. But if enough people value it, then it represents a service enhancement.

Improved value for the customer comes from lower costs or better service. The latter comes in many shapes and forms. All are substantive and measurable. Better service can be measured in terms of lower or more precise lead times, improved after-sales service, greater variety, better purchase processes, and a multitude of other aspects of performance.

For the producer or supplier, it results in greater price realization, higher margins, and increased volume.

So, despite what much of the literature on customer service suggests, customer care is not only about mind-set, culture change, or being nice. Only by first figuring out how to optimize value for the customer can a supplier determine the channel's roles. The trouble is that the typical interaction focuses on the supplier's desires rather than the channel's desires. It is astonishing to observe the number of companies embroiled in vigorous, long-standing internal debates about who their customer is—the channel or the end user. It's easy to opt for the channel as the channel representatives are the ones the supplier hears from most regularly, but it's not necessarily a wise choice. And once the consumer relationship is relinquished to the channel, in an act of appeasement by the supplier, it is hard to reclaim. You only have to look at what has happened with supermarkets in recent years to see this at work. The introduction of own-label products (often manufactured by the same suppliers who make the leading brands) and retailer loyalty programs has made supermarket stores some of the most dominant channels in retailing. They have more information—not just on what consumers purchase but on how they purchase—than manufacturers and they increasingly exert their influence in areas such as category management. Effectively, the manufacturers have surrendered power to the supermarkets.

Aside from the power struggles, the reality is straightforward:

*Successful companies identify and target the few dimensions of service that customers really value and pay for.*

By contrast, companies that are unsuccessful tend to have spent money too broadly in a shotgun approach to improving service. Often, they have essentially bribed their channel to provide better service. As with most service improvement programs, the results tend to be disappointing since the underlying drivers of customer value are not affected.

Typically with the latter, good performers in the channel are paid for what they are already doing, while poor performers only undertake short-lived, superficial steps to make their customers happy.

For example, one luxury car manufacturer discovered that its program of financial incentives to motivate dealers to improve service had little substantive impact. The manufacturer found that what distinguished the better dealers was their higher performance in the more difficult areas of customer satisfaction. These included fixing a car right the first time, maintaining an acceptable level of parts availability, and keeping the quality of the service work performed uniformly high. The manufacturer's financial inducements had virtually no effect on the drivers of satisfaction. The better dealers were already striving in these areas, and those performing poorly had neither the instinct nor the ability to alter their behavior. Instead, this latter group, when prompted, was inclined to focus on factors that had less leverage with customers. In other words, a pleasant service adviser cannot compensate for a car that is not fixed right the first time. Again, this stems from confusing a friendly smile with good service.

*The reality is that the channel as a whole is unlikely to make fundamental changes without concerted, focused assistance.*

At this point, corporate cynics are likely to suggest that herein lies the problem. Concerted, focused assistance, they are likely to suggest, does not come cheap. The customer may end up happier but only at additional cost to the extended enterprise, and mostly to the supplier. Increased satisfaction is assumed to require increased service, which is presumed to cost more. This may be true of the broad, superficial efforts. However, customer care programs focused on a few key drivers of value for selected segments of the market usually result in major efficiency gains. And those gains can—and should—offset any additional costs.

For example, in 1996 Chase Manhattan Bank and Wal-Mart unveiled their cobranded MasterCard. It attracted a million account customers in its first year. "Having our own credit card lowers our credit card processing costs. This provides us with another way of passing savings on to our customers," said Wal-Mart director of specialty marketing,

Peggy Knight. The credit card was another opportunity to provide value to customers.[2]

To target critical elements that can create true value, customer care programs must consider the economics of serving customers. This understanding is used to identify redundant or low-value activities and to flag opportunities that have attractive returns. As a result, well-directed programs should lead to lower costs and higher revenues or margins.

# Channel Power

There is no great mystery to the stories of Snap-on, Southwest, or Lexus. They are companies that have recognized that service and channel management are critical to success.

But how do they make that realization work for them? How do they convert a good idea into bottom-line results? As we have noted, channels are the routes to and relationships with customers. To maximize the benefits, companies have to start with an understanding of channels. Channels basically consist of three functions:

- Information flow from suppliers to end customers and vice versa
- Logistics to get the supplier's products to the end customer
- Value-added services that augment the supplier's product

**Information Flow**

In general, better, more readily available, and cheaper information yields more sophisticated and more demanding channel players and end customers. From customer back to manufacturer and in the reverse direction, information flow is central to the channel management process. "Businesses are increasingly competing on the basis of information," says Ben Barnes, general manager of IBM's global business intelligence unit.[3]

Information basically flows in two directions. First, there is outbound information about the supplier's offering through advertising and promotional literature, and then there is inbound information about the needs of customers, coming (among other sources) from customer satisfaction surveys and studies of buying and ownership behaviors. Effective

## Channel Champions: Snap-on Uniqueness

Service adds value and usually comes with one great advantage: it is harder to copy than product features. You may be able to identify every single ingredient in a Big Mac, but you can't readily replicate the service and culture that surrounds the product. A camera manufacturer may be able to copy a smart new extra function introduced by a competitor with relative ease. It is far harder to respond to a new service offering.

For example, look at the success of the Snap-on Tools Corporation. Founded in 1920, Snap-on invented its own channel for selling high-quality tools and equipment for the automotive industry. From its headquarters in Kenosha, Wisconsin, the company has built a thriving business by bypassing the traditional retail channel. It offers high-quality products to customers via franchise dealers who operate from their own mobile stores.

Today, the company's famous white trucks—retail outlets on wheels—are a common sight not just in the United States but in many countries around the world. Stocked with $100,000 of inventory, Snap-on's 5,700 franchise dealers drive their mobile stores to car dealerships, service stations, independent garages—the places where mechanics and car enthusiasts are to be found. An additional 325 trucks are driven by Snap-on's own technical representatives, who provide training and technical backup to the dealers in the field.

The Snap-on business model is deceptively simple. Each franchise dealer owns the truck-based store and works a private patch on a rota basis so that customers know when to expect the next visit. "The whole corporation is based on one thing," one veteran dealer told researcher and author Glen Rifkin, "all the dealers getting up in the morning, getting behind the steering wheel and seeing that first customer. It's all face-to-face, one-to-one."[4]

Snap-on's lifeblood is an ongoing relationship between the franchise holder and the customer. In essence, what Snap-on has created is a channel based on a web of personal relationships. What the company realized long before its competitors was that its customers—typically mechanics in the United States and, in Europe, independent garage-owners—didn't have time to leave their workplace to buy tools. They were prepared to pay a premium price to have good quality tools delivered to their doors.

| COMPANY | Snap-on Incorporated | |
|---|---|---|
| Subsidiaries include | Hein-Werner Corporation | |
| ADDRESS | 10801 Corporate Drive, Kenosha WI 53141–1430 USA Phone: 414–656–5200   Fax: 414–656–5577 URL: http://www.snapon.com | |
| BUSINESS | Tools | |
| STATISTICS | Employees | 1997   11,700 |
| | Annual sales (mil) | 1998   $1,773 |
| | Annual results (mil) | 1998   $111.9 (excluding one-time charges) |
| | Other facts | Snap-on markets its products in 150 countries plus, through more than 6,000 dealers. |

What mattered to them was that they could rely on the quality of the products they needed to make a living.

But it is the mix of three factors that makes the channel effective. The winning combination is quality, plus easy credit terms that allow mechanics to afford premium products, plus the accessibility of mobile stores and friendly dealers.

While Snap-on remains committed to an army of loyal customers, it would be wrong to think the company has an old-fashioned vision. Its strategy is to build on its existing channel to become the one-stop store for car mechanics, catering to all their needs.

In recent years, the company has made a number of acquisitions to assimilate products and expertise and to extend its capabilities into areas such as software-based diagnostics systems and management information systems. According to the company's chairman and CEO, Robert A. Cornog, the aim has been to integrate all of its capabilities into a single computerized system

Channel Champions: Snap-on Uniqueness (continued)

(launched in 1997). Snap-on will know more about vehicles over their life cycle than many manufacturers, creating value in improving product designs and repair operations.

Snap-on has now successfully moved into the diagnostic market. Its channel management has proved highly robust. Mutual respect between the company and its customers is genuine and long-established. But, clearly, respect is unusual. To date, no one has successfully copied Snap-on.

*Channels the Snap-on Way*

- *Snap-on is much more than product.* Its offering is made up of a combination of services provided through a variety of channels. It is the guy in the truck you get to know. It is the credit he provides, which helps your cash flow. And it is the product.
- *Know yourself.* CEO Cornog regards the company as an upscale retail operation disguised as a manufacturer.
- *High product quality; high service quality.* Snap-on has built an image based on functionality, reliability, and high quality. To tool lovers, the Snap-on brand has the same sort of cachet as Mercedes Benz or Cartier. With its image of understated excellence, it is the choice of the discerning mechanic who, in turn, is prepared to pay thousands of dollars for Snap-on tools and the storage accessories such as cases, carts, and chests to keep them ready for use. High quality is matched by convenience and reliability.
- *Creative financing to build relationships.* Unlike the affluent consumers who buy premier branded luxury goods such as fashion accessories and perfumes, Snap-on's customers are distinctly blue collar. They are in the lower-to-middle-income bracket with limited access to credit. Realizing this, Snap-on offers financial services as an essential component of its selling proposition. Its dealers began offering credit to customers back in the Depression. Snap-on dealers continue to offer interest-free credit on most sales. Through its financial services arm, too, the company offers loans for more expensive equipment. These are interest-bearing loans, but they are available to customers who would have difficulty obtaining credit elsewhere.

## Channel Champions: Herb's Love In

Copying service excellence is like trying to copy a five-line Picasso drawing: straightforward until you try it. You might think that the Snap-on example is an exceptional case: a company creates a new channel and maintains service excellence in a fairly humdrum business. The competitors don't come running because there aren't that many in the first place and even fewer with the money, infrastructure, or gusto to compete with the first one on the field.

This is only partly true. In fact, Snap-on's success in the channel it created is due to sound management that ensures that its advantage remains secure and is not taken for granted. If you invent a channel and manage it well, your competitive advantage can prove surprisingly resilient. To help prove our case, we next look at a familiar industry, air travel, and the astounding success of Herb Kelleher's Southwest Airlines in one of the most cutthroat and intensely competitive markets in the world.

Over twenty-seven years, Southwest has stamped an indelible mark on the industry. Herb Kelleher has proved that service differentiation is a CEO-level issue. "It is still the low-cost airline

| **COMPANY** | **Southwest Airlines Co.** | |
|---|---|---|
| **ADDRESS** | 2702 Love Field Drive, Dallas TX 75235 USA<br>Phone: 214–792–4000   Fax: 214–792–5015<br><br>URL: http://www.southwest.com | |
| **BUSINESS** | Air travel | |
| **STATISTICS** | Employees | 1997    23,974 |
| | Annual sales (mil) | 1998    $4,164 |
| | Annual results (mil) | 1998    $433 |
| | Other facts | SWA has a turned in a twenty-five-year run of profits—without any strikes. It provides 2,300 flights to fifty U.S. cities in twenty-five states daily. |

Channel Champions: Herb's Love In (continued)

by which all others are judged," notes the *Financial Times*.[5] Yet if you look at the basics, Southwest doesn't appear to have a lot going for it. Its product, from a businessperson's perspective, seems inferior. There is no first class, no seat assignment. This is the kind of thing that matters to harried businesspeople anxious to pull out the laptop and finish a report during the flight. Yet Southwest still captures a reasonable share of business traffic. Its services are high frequency, punctual, and well located—Southwest reduces passengers' ground journeys by flying to alternative airports. The value of this higher certainty and shorter overall door-to-door time is immeasurable to many business travelers. On top of this is the legendary, much-talked-about Southwest service, which is built around people who enjoy their work and enjoy helping customers. Southwest started wooing customers—male ones at least—with a "Love" theme (drinks became Love Potions and so on). Now, it does so through its promise of "positively outrageous service."

In a business that is often bland, Southwest sends out strong, simple messages to customers and employees—this adds value for both groups. This information flow combines to help the company's logistics. Turnaround times tend to be quicker than those of competitors—often twenty minutes—because staff work together.

Again, it is nothing like rocket science. But it gave Southwest a huge head start. It invented a new channel—low thrills, low cost, high service—and, as a result, captured the Texas market and built up a tidy cash pile to expand into other plum markets such as California. Now the seventh-biggest carrier in the United States, Southwest has a long record—twenty-four years—of uninterrupted in-the-black performance. Others have, inevitably, boarded the bandwagon. United has attempted to "rise higher" and the latest no-thrills airline, Go, comes from British Airways. They have a lot of catching up to do.

*Channels by Southwest*

- *Old products can be delivered in new ways*. The airline business is nothing new. Yet Southwest reinvented it as a new experience.

- *Service differentiation is difficult to emulate.* Many have tried and are still trying to match Southwest's levels of customer service; few if any have managed to achieve it.
- *Continuous service excellence demands a strong corporate culture.* A temporary period of brilliant service can be the result of sending a few employees on a development program. But only a genuinely customer-centered corporate culture can really deliver continuous service excellence.
- *Focus on a few key dimensions of customer satisfaction.* In their battle to get their seats right, airlines often forget that satisfied customers are pleased by simple things. Continental's revival under Gordon Bethune was given impetus and direction by his simple insistence that its planes be punctual.
- *Focus on a particular segment of the market.* Southwest was the first airline to segment the market according to service. It understood what its target customers really wanted and then created an organization that delivered it time and time again.
- *Customer service is a boardroom issue.* The lead comes from Herb Kelleher. He acts as the living reminder of the company's culture.

## Channel Champions: The Lexus Ownership Experience

Launched in 1989, the Lexus was initially greeted as a triumph for Japanese imitation. The public relations line was that the Lexus was "unlike any other car in the world." Media pundits laughed at the company's effrontery—"The LS400 had Mercedes S-class wannabe stamped on every panel and part," said one critic. "If Toyota could have slapped a Mercedes star on the front of the Lexus, it would have fooled most of the people most of the time."

The reality is more complex. The Lexus did not compete on the basis of product similarity. If so, it would surely have failed. In fact, Toyota tackled something of an imponderable in the car industry. The received wisdom was that the top brands had the higher end of the market sewn up. Brand loyalty to BMW or Mercedes was very strong, and any interloper would surely fail. A straight copy of a Mercedes would not have worked, in the same way as a copy of a Jaguar or a BMW would have proved unsuccessful. The Lexus resembled a Mercedes, but Toyota threw everything its people could think of at it. (As noted earlier, Toyota is keen to tell you that the Lexus took seven years, $2 billion, 1,400 engineers, 2,300 technicians, and 450 prototypes, and generated 200 patents.) Toyota effectively took the quality

| COMPANY | Lexus Division | |
|---|---|---|
| ADDRESS | 19001 S. Western Avenue, Torrance CA 90501 USA<br>P.O. Box 2991, Torrance CA 90509<br>Phone: 310–328–2075<br><br>URL: http://www.lexus.com/homepage/homepage1/ | |
| BUSINESS | Automobile | |
| STATISTICS | Annual sales (mil) | 1998    $5,500 (estimate) |
| | Other facts | Lexus Division is a subsidiary of Toyota Motor Sales USA. |

standards and moved them forward. It moved the goalposts. If Mercedes and BMW could boast of engineering excellence, Toyota set out to outdo them, or at least overpower them with sheer excess. Toyota, for example, made great play of the fact that the car was tested in Japan on mile after mile of carefully built highways that exactly imitated roads in the United States, Germany, or the United Kingdom. Toyota even put in the right road signs. Toyota made it easier for potential customers to buy its product. It looked right. It oozed quality. It was the same, but different enough to warrant examination. And it was initially priced well below (10 percent to 20 percent below) the relevant competition.

While the product stood up to scrutiny, where Lexus really stole a march on its rivals was through the Lexus ownership experience. Even when things went wrong, the service was excellent. An early problem led to a product recall. Lexus had dealers call up people personally and immediately. Instead of having a negative effect, the recall strengthened the channel. Lexus encountered a product problem like many others do, but the up-front, customer-oriented manner in which they addressed the problem was differentiating.

Because of the high profit potential of an exclusive dealership, new networks such as Lexus and Saturn can be extremely selective in granting franchises so as to choose dealers who offer very high levels of customer service. Both have extraordinarily stringent selection criteria, especially in the area of customer satisfaction—they look for dealers with the proper mind-set. Across the United States, Lexus chose one hundred thirty dealers out of ten thousand applicants. For one market area examined, Saturn chose one dealer out of seventy-two applicants.

Lexus interviews and surveys all employees. For every dealership, it surveys hundreds of customers to gauge how they were treated and how satisfied they are. Lexus and Saturn use operating guidelines and regular customer surveys to monitor dealer performance against customer satisfaction criteria. Lexus and Saturn monitor customer satisfaction and provide monthly feedback to dealers; they also have operating guidelines and training to help dealers. Poor performance results in factory personnel visits to assess the problem and prescribe remedies. Perhaps the most unusual thing is that both offer only moderate financial incentives for achieving high levels of customer satisfaction, and there are no explicit contractual provisions on customer satisfaction levels.

The message is that customer satisfaction is expected. It is good business. The dealers naturally view superior customer service as one of the differentiating features that enables them to generate high levels of customer loyalty and continued success.

Nonetheless, Lexus almost became a victim of its own success. The new dealer network was highly successful with much larger margins than enjoyed by other dealers. There were lengthy waiting lists for the product. Lexus told its dealers that it was leasing 40 percent of its new cars and expected this figure to rise to 60 percent to 70 percent.

This was the good news. And the bad news? In three years there would be a glut of used Lexuses in the market. This was bad news for dealers: who wants a car that doesn't hold its value and who buys a new car when second-hand ones are so cheap? It was even worse news for owners—in three years their cars would not be worth a great deal.

Lexus had to take action because the residual value risk was so large. The company needed to discover a way of ensuring that the cars remained under its control. It didn't want dealers to send them to auction en masse to produce an abundance of heavily discounted used models in the market. This would inevitably mean that Lexus would have to offer discounts and the whole system would fall apart. Its aim, therefore, was to improve the resale value of the car.

Lexus's solution was to introduce a Certified Pre-Owned Vehicle Program, which sought to cut out the uncertainty of buying a used car. (Others had tried a similar approach with undistinguished results—Jaguar and Mercedes had established used-car programs but neither was working very well.) The program involved advertising to build awareness, a 100-point inspection program ("both mechanical and aesthetic"), reconditioning standards, conditions for dealers (for example, they couldn't carry certified and uncertified cars on the same lot). Lexus also set up an Internet dealer remarketing system so dealers could meet supply and demand imbalances. (In the United States used cars generally migrate from the Northeast to the Southwest.) The beauty of all this was that instead of a trade-off, Toyota achieved a transfer of incentives so that a win-win situation was created. Customers' used vehicle prices were propped up, which in turn supported new car prices and values for Lexus. In terms of value creation, through their used vehicle certification programs, Lexus and Toyota rank among the highest of all vehicle manufacturers. This value creation has as much to do with the channel management as with the product itself, or more.

## Channels by Lexus

- *The Lexus is more than a product.* It is an entire ownership experience. Toyota's realization was that selling an expensive car is not only about selling the metal box. The product is the point of entry to a relationship with potential customers. Service delivered through the channel is the basis of that relationship.
- *Dealer selection is key.* Lexus hired people who thought about customer service. They aren't just pushing cars. As a result, it didn't offer special financial incentives to motivate dealers. People are either inclined to understand that truly good customer service creates value for customers and dealers or they are not. They either like talking to customers and sorting out their concerns and problems, or they do not. There is no middle ground.

two-way information flow—as with the best of the current e-commerce players—creates mutual understanding and, eventually, a bond of loyalty between supplier and customer that is hard to break.

Historically, much of the flow of information has usually been left to the channel to manage. Channel players have the most direct contact with consumers to provide information and to gather the best information about end customers.

In the grocery industry, for example, companies have used consumer-specific information—and continue to do so through such initiatives as customized coupons at the checkout stand. Indeed, manufacturers often know surprisingly little about the people who actually use their products and as a result are forced to treat channel players as customers. In many cases, manufacturers only address end customers through broad-based marketing strategies such as image and brand advertising.

Look, for example, at the traditional approach in the automotive industry, where manufacturers have had very little interaction with customers. Responsibility was abdicated to the dealerships and companies tended not to know who bought what or where. The somewhat confrontational relationship between dealers and manufacturers hasn't helped. The situation is changing.

Now, information flow is more critical than ever. New Internet-based intermediaries are leveraging independent automobile product, service, and price information, which weakens manufacturers' and dealers' relationships with customers. Car makers are investing millions of dollars on systems and processes to help them learn more about and from their customers. As we move from product to service-based differentiation, companies have to understand things they didn't traditionally understand or even know about. And, what's more, they then have to manage them.

Manufacturers can no longer wash their hands and delegate information gathering. They often have the scale advantages to gather and employ customer information for strategic and tactical purposes. For example, data mining is an increasingly important technique for understanding consumers and developing channels tailored to their needs. In contrast, channel players often have too limited a perspective and too broad a product scope to build deep knowledge of customers' product-specific needs.

Little wonder then that observing customers has become a science—and an industry. Dorothy Leonard identifies four types of information available from observing customers:[6]

- The triggers that prompt people to use a product or service
- The relationship between the product and the consumer's environment
- The ways consumers customize the product (and so how manufacturers can make those modifications for them)
- The intangible qualities consumers value in the product

The important thing is not so much which product or service customers buy but how they buy and how they interact with the product and the channel through which it is delivered. Such is the power of observation that Steelcase, the office furniture company, used observational research to reposition itself as a company that understood work processes rather than a simple manufacturer.

Chrysler used observation in the product development of its minivan. Rather than traditional market research, it watched women using station wagons and found that additional space was required by "soccer moms" making multiple stops hauling children, daily purchases, and other equipment. Ford is now also using a range of nontraditional market research techniques to identify future customer needs.

There is growing recognition that information can be gathered in a myriad of useful ways.

Car company Daewoo has a database of customers. Every time the company touches a customer the database is updated. It can build a relationship despite the fact that it has outsourced the traditional vehicle servicing element to a third party.

Jeffrey Rayport and John Sviokla of Harvard Business School have examined the performance of Frito Lay in this area. Frito is one of a growing number of companies that have honed the logistics of operations and, in particular, of information gathering to a fine art. "Frito's employees in the field collect information on the sales of products daily, store by store across the nation, and feed it electronically to the company. The employees also collect information about the sales and promotions of competing products or about new products launched by competitors in select locations," they report.

"By combining this field data with information from each stage of the value chain, Frito's managers can better determine levels of in-bound supplies of raw materials, allocate the company's manufacturing activity across available production capacity, and plan truck routing for the most efficient coverage of market areas. The company's ability to target local demand patterns with just the right sales promotion means that it can continuously optimize margin in the face of inventory risk. In short, Frito can use information to see and react to activities along its physical value chain."[7] Frito uses information flow to ensure that it manages the channel as effectively as possible.

Clearly, technology has had an immense impact in information flow. Technology means that companies can know more about their customers than ever before—and vice versa. The Internet has opened up entirely new vistas. Jonathan Reynolds of Oxford University's Templeton College argues that, for many established companies, an entry-level presence for doing business on the Internet might be a purely informational one that complements existing promotional activity—combining, perhaps, on-line press releases with an annual report. This is a low-risk but low-reward strategy.[8]

More imaginative are corporations that seek to provide information important to their customers. Inchcape Shipping, for example, provided summaries of port information to its customers.

## Logistics

The second function of channels is effective logistics, transporting—physically or electronically—the product and service to the customer. Some companies have built their businesses around the efficient management of logistics—both to the customer and back to suppliers.

Until the media and financial information giant Reuters introduced the first electronic dealing system in the 1970s, the service—which amounted to on-line access to financial information—did not exist. The creation of this new channel effectively gave Reuters a competitive advantage in its market, paralleling the company's pioneering use of the telegraph to transmit news years before. Explains Martin Davids, a senior technology manager at Reuters: "We didn't get where we are today by doing what

## Using EDI

A forerunner of e-commerce, Electronic Data Interchange has already had a major impact on channel management. EDI uses networked computer systems to connect all parts the value chain. So, for example, it can create an efficient channel of information running between suppliers, manufacturers, and retailers. This means that wasteful inefficiency in inventory management, ordering, shipping, and invoicing can all be reduced.

EDI enables retailers or distributors to place orders directly into the manufacturer's system. This cuts administrative costs and reduces overall inventory levels in the system. Since the retailer–distributor must integrate its systems with the manufacturer's to some extent for EDI to work, it also creates switching costs for the retailer–distributor—a benefit for the manufacturer.

Beyond this, however, EDI systems also mean that timely and accurate data can be used to improve decision making, and to track the behavior and buying patterns of customers.

EDI is also used to get closer to customers. It has played a critical role in the Efficient Customer Response (ECR) movement. The ECR Europe Executive Board—made up of a group of leading retailers and manufacturers including Tesco, Safeway, Nestlé, Unilever, and Procter & Gamble—predicts that the application of ECR in Europe could generate savings in the grocery supply chain equivalent to an average 5.7 percent price reduction. This, they believe, can be achieved through its implementation in eight areas:

- High scanning accuracy
- Automated store ordering
- Continuous replenishment
- Optimized promotions (based on accurate customer information)
- Assortment planning
- Reliable operations
- Synchronized production
- Integrated suppliers

One of the pioneers of EDI was Wal-Mart. In the late eighties, Wal-Mart suppliers such as Wrangler and GE were using vendor-managed inventory systems to replenish stocks in Wal-Mart stores and warehouses. By using IT applications such as cash register scanners, Wal-Mart can now gain a detailed understanding of customers' habits and preferences. This information is then fed back up the channel to suppliers who are told what to produce in what quantities and where to ship it to. Over 3,500 suppliers of Wal-Mart's have on-line access to information about their products in Wal-Mart's database and can analyze buying patterns.[9]

Warehousing and inventory is greatly reduced as a result. This allows the company to use 10 percent of its available space for storage compared to the 25 percent average of its competitors. "Every cost, every time is carefully analyzed, enabling better merchandising decisions to be made on a daily basis," says Randy Mott, senior vice president in charge of information systems.[10]

Wal-Mart is now using data mining software to detect patterns at its 2,400 U.S. stores. The aim, according to Rob Fusillo, director of replenishment systems, is to manage inventories "one store at a time, like [each store] was its own dedicated chain."[11] In fact, Wal-Mart possesses the world's largest data warehouse, containing a massive twenty-four terabytes of data.

The process of information gathering begins at the point of sale. Wal-Mart captures point-of-sale transaction information from each of its outlets and moves it through its network to its data warehouse at HQ in Bentonville, Arkansas. The information is then queried if necessary and sales trends analyzed by item and by store. This enables the company to make decisions about replenishment, customer buying trends, seasonal buying trends. The aim is to get the right products to the right store at the right time. "Our business strategy depends on detailed data at every level," says Randy Mott. "Every cost, every line item is carefully analyzed enabling better merchandising decisions to be made on a daily basis."

Of course, the bottom line is what you do with the information acquired. While there is a profusion of available information, this does not mean that companies necessarily use the information effectively once it is gathered. Estimates vary, but it is suggested by some that businesses only use between 7 percent and 10 percent of the data they have accumulated.[12] More is better only if it helps build insights that allow better decisions to be made. The role of more sophisticated decision support systems, driven by data and analytic models, to manage channel activities is dramatically rising.

our customers wanted. All the big products that make all the money, apart from the basic data delivery stuff, nobody thought they wanted. Some of them said at the beginning, in the case of the dealing system, that they didn't want it at all. So in a sense we created new markets."[13]

In fact, what the company did was to create a brand new channel for delivering its product—information—and new ways for the customers in the dealing rooms to use it.

Logistics now involves efficient utilization of information from and to customers and suppliers. In Japan, 7-Eleven has become the country's largest retailer through the use of information-gathering technology to create an efficient logistics system. Few retailers can match its analytical zeal. Each store—and there are over 6,800 in Japan—has a point-of-sale computer linked to headquarters. The computer tells the store manager about sales data, demographic trends, and even weather forecasts. The manager is expected to use all the analytical tools available—and those who don't will receive a friendly warning from the company.[14]

Distribution hubs divide products into four categories depending on temperature, and deliver them on schedules ranging from three times a day for the core fast-food products to once a week for canned goods. This cuts the number of separate deliveries to each store from about seventy to ten a day, timed to bring in supplies of fast-moving foods just before peak demand periods.[15]

One vital aspect of the logistics function of channels is the efficient management of inventory. According to a study by the *Harvard Business Review,* the cost of carrying inventory for a year is equivalent to at least a quarter of the price retailers pay for the product. As a result, a two-week inventory reduction represents a cost saving of nearly 1 percent of sales.

Again, inventory control is something at which Dell excels. Dell's efficient use of technology to reduce inventory has enabled the company to create a new business model. Dell's method of selling to individual customers and building products to order has become known as the "direct model." It is a form of what Michael Dell labels "virtual integration." This harnesses the economic benefits of two very different business models. It offers the advantages of a tightly coordinated supply chain that have traditionally come through vertical integration. At the same time, it benefits from the focus and specialization that drive single-product corporations.

"When the company started, I don't think we knew how far the direct model could take us. It has provided a consistent underlying strategy for Dell despite a lot of change in our industry. Along the way, we have learned a lot, and the model has evolved," says Dell. "Most important, the direct model has allowed us to leverage our relationships with both suppliers and customers to such an extent that I believe it's fair to think of our companies as being virtually integrated."[16]

Managing inventory is essential to Dell's approach. The effective sharing of information has allowed Dell to reduce stored components to just eleven days of inventory. Inventory levels and replenishment needs are constantly relayed. Some vendors are in communication with Dell every hour. According to Michael Dell, the key challenge lies in changing the focus from *how much* inventory there is to *how fast* it is moving. "In our industry, if you can get people to think about how fast inventory is moving, then you create real value. Why? Because if I've got 11 days of inventory and my competitor has 80, and Intel comes out with a new 450-megahertz chip, that means I'm going to get to market 69 days sooner."[17]

Dell is not alone. In a completely different industry, electrical products distribution, Houston Wire and Cable (HWC) has created a dominant logistics capability to supply a focused product line. HWC is now the national leader in the distribution of wire and cable in the United States. It stocks 50,000 SKUs of wire and cable while a typical electrical distributor carries about 20,000 individual products, or stock-keeping units (SKUs), in a variety of lines. HWC's sales and logistics capabilities are uniquely tailored to serve its specific market. It has a state-of-the-art, real-time inventory management system that features round-the-clock order taking and has led to unmatched fill rates. Advanced systems link the company to vendors and customers electronically and link different HWC locations. In addition, salespeople know exactly how many feet of wire there are on each reel and are given special bonuses for selling the end of a reel. HWC customers and end users have access to extensive technical support.

The result of these various initiatives is that HWC achieved growth of 15 percent per year with an operating margin of greater than 9 percent (ROS greater than 5 percent) and 2.5 asset turns—a performance far superior to virtually all others in the industry.

### Value-Added Services

The final function of channels is to provide a market for services that are additions to the basic product or service offering. These now come in a myriad of forms including local selling, financing, customization, and after-sales parts and service.

A host of sales and after-sales services now accompany almost every product or service. And it doesn't matter what business you are in.

HWC, for example, sells cable management services—it will manage all a customer's cable needs for a project, minimize scrap, and buy back the unused portions.

New Pig Corporation in Tipton, Pennsylvania, makes industrial absorbents. Its products soak up grease and spillages in factories. The company has over three hundred employees and anticipated 1998 sales of $77 million, and is growing at a healthy annual rate of 10 percent.

New Pig's success was initially based on branding and innovative products. Prior to the development of absorbent socks, spillages were usually dealt with by piling sand on top of them. This made a mess and didn't actually solve the problem.

The pig-lie sock did. The company grew rapidly.

A clever blend of quality products and piggy branding has been bringing home the bacon ever since. It has transformed what might otherwise have been a bland industrial cleaning firm into a marketing phenomenon. There is, the company cheerfully admits, nothing particularly clever or strategic about its brand or its business formula. It takes unglamourous but useful products and adds some hoggy humor.

Take a typical New Pig product—an absorbent mat that can be put around a machine to soak up spills. In New Pig's capable trotters, it becomes the altogether more interesting Ham-O PIG Mat—complete with a colorful piggy pattern and slogan ("tough as a pig's hide") and a cartoon pig dressed in piggy overalls. "There's not a market in the world where people don't like to laugh and have fun and be treated as important customers," observes company cofounder and chairman, Ben Stapelfeld.[18]

New Pig appeared to be doing everything right. It grew steadily and was featured in rankings of the fastest-growing private companies. But not all was well. "Life was wonderful but we were too busy doing what we needed to do rather than thinking about what we should be doing.

We were working hard but not being that smart," says Ben Stapelfeld. "It took us a long time to realize that we were a big player in a $250 million market." The unacknowledged trouble was that New Pig's market was in fast-declining manufacturing. The company sold products cleverly and successfully but the market appeared limited and future growth potential constrained.

So the company looked at itself. It reckoned it was good at customer service. Then it called in some consultants who pointed out that New Pig was good at measuring various aspects of its performance—how many times the phones rang before they were answered—but not actually very good at listening to what was important to customers.

As a result, New Pig has shifted its emphasis away from selling products to offering solutions and building customer relationships. Alastair McSkimming of New Pig's U.K. operation explains: "There is an overtone of humor but our products solve people's problems. So, we now provide people with information on safety and technical standards and carry out site assessments. We are there to help people solve problems rather than to make a sale." Ben Stapelfeld says: "We're about keeping plants clean. That's a huge market not a $250 million one. We are changing the definition of what we are."[19]

Value-added services change customers' perceptions of what you are there for. They change the nature of their relationship with you and, as a result, change the nature of the channel.

Value-added services can come in the form of entertainment, apparent diversions to the main experience—but ones that nevertheless add real value to the experience. From its earliest days, the Swedish furniture company IKEA recognized the importance of channel management—going to great lengths to create a bundle of value-added services around its stores that fit with its guiding philosophy. Operating through out-of-town sites to keep costs down, the company relies on customers' being prepared to travel to its stores. Building on its early experience in Sweden—when a visit to an IKEA store could involve a day's travel—IKEA aims to make shopping an enjoyable experience rather than a chore. This has enabled IKEA to succeed in taking its formula to the United States, an effort where many European retailers have failed.

As Sven Kuldorf, vice president of IKEA of Sweden (part of the IKEA group), explains: "The only way of keeping the customer long-term in our vision is that the customer has a benefit from coming to IKEA. The product and price quality that we offer must be the best. We even say that we must have better prices than our competitors as one of our operating principles. That is basic to our long-term success."

While product-based differentiation is regarded as the foundation of the business, more interesting is the edifice built on this base. It is a business built not around products per se but around a distinctive shopping experience. "From there we say how can we make a visit to IKEA a day out. IKEA should be a day out. That started in the first store here in Almhult," says Sven Kuldorf. "In the old days to come to our store they had to leave early in the morning. For an average customer the journey would take a couple of hours and many of our customers had small children. So we have had crèches [to look after customers' young children] for a very long time, and facilities for children, and then we have the restaurants. We believe that the prices should be very good so that customers with young families should be able to afford to eat there and not have to bring sandwiches. They shouldn't have to leave IKEA just because they are hungry. We don't have entertainers every day but very often on Saturdays and Sundays we will have a clown or things like that." The *experience* is the IKEA thing: service differentiates one shelving unit from another.

# The Channel Management Process

We believe there has been an important shift in power. Channels are increasingly important. How companies manage their three key functions—information flow, logistics, and value-added services—is crucial.

Product and service suppliers have a number of possible responses to this shift in power:

First, they may choose to do nothing. This will mean that the winning channels will increase their margins and control at the expense of suppliers and losing channels. It is not an option.

Adding value is not about a few added extras at the periphery. The Saturn automobile is a prime example of the shift in emphasis away from tangible product attribute-based value to "soft" and service-based differentiation. It is also an object lesson in how value-added services can fundamentally alter the customer–supplier relationship.

The Saturn was launched in 1990 and was GM's first new nameplate since Chevrolet. The car itself is fairly spartan. Most persuasively, the Saturn is backed by a terrific dealer network that provides truly differentiated sales with no haggling, as well as high-quality service. (So inconsistent were the standards in the auto business that loaners and car washes used to be jewels in Saturn's service crown.)

Saturn has laid out what it calls its "pricing principles": "No hassle means Saturn Retailers are up-front about all elements of

| COMPANY | Saturn Corporation | |
|---|---|---|
| ADDRESS | 1420 Stephenson Hwy., Troy MI 48083<br>P.O. Box 7025, Troy MI 48007<br>Phone: 248–524–5000<br><br>URL: http://www.saturncars.com/index.html<br>http://www.gm.com/ | |
| BUSINESS | Automobile | |
| STATISTICS | Employees | 1998    9,600 |
| | Other facts | Saturn is a subsidiary of General Motors |

a vehicle's price. No last minute add-ons or hidden charges. Nothing up our sleeves. No haggle means the retailer should stick to whatever price it sets. Horse trading and dickering don't fit with Saturn's philosophy: No Customer should ever wonder whether the Retailer's next Customer will get a better price by 'driving a harder bargain.'"[20]

Saturn demonstrates the use of service as a differentiator of an undistinguished product—once again, it is a differentiator that competitors have so far failed to copy successfully.

None of this is accidental. As we've already noted, Saturn's brand development focused on the buying experience, service, and support—on the people and the processes, rather than on the product.

According to research by J.D. Power, the three car brands in the United States with the highest customer satisfaction are Lexus, Infiniti, and Saturn. The link between them is that all have *de novo* dealer networks designed, developed, and managed with an intense pursuit of consistent, exceptional customer service.

In 1996, the Saturn was rated best in overall sales satisfaction among all car brands. It was rated seventh in customer satisfaction—and the top six were all luxury cars that offered far more by way of in-the-seat rewards: Lexus, Infiniti, Acura, Mercedes-Benz, Cadillac, and Jaguar.

Customers even gave Saturn high marks on the service they received when their cars were recalled.[21]

Contrast this with the problems GM has experienced elsewhere with dealerships featuring a variety of its models. In 1995, GM vice president Ronald L. Zarrella wrote to 8,500 dealers pointing out, rather belatedly, that its autos were not commodities and offering them for sale next to competing brands was not what GM wanted. It was significant that while there are 8,500 U.S. GM dealerships, there are 17,000 franchises. Individual dealers can have as many as six franchises operating from the same place. Saturn dealers have no such complications. Their emphasis on straight talking and value-added service remains distinctive.

## Channel Champions: Service with Saturn (continued)

### Channels by Saturn

- *Beyond products.* Saturn is not really just a car. It is a low-hassle transportation service. It is low-hassle to buy, low-hassle to maintain. The product is not unique. It is hardly differentiated from the mass of other cars on offer.
- *Customer-friendly shopping.* A sales strategy that creates a customer-friendly shopping and buying experience. The no-haggle pricing policy and money-back guarantee are only part of this. It was a brand new dealer network. But what many people don't mention is that most Saturn dealers have other dealerships. They are now conforming to Saturn's standards. It is doing what makes sense and getting it right.
- *Selling the image.* The focus is on selling the company image instead of pushing a car as in other companies. As part of this, the Saturn sales force conducts follow-up calls with new customers to answer questions and ensure satisfaction.
- *No saturation.* A market area concept that avoids proliferating dealerships and significantly limits in-line competition, allowing the no-haggle pricing policy to stick.
- *Training and incentives.* A commitment to investing in its employees through training and incentives. Each employee receives 170 hours of training each year, in which all executives, including the CEO, provide instruction. It is an explicit company goal to compensate fairly and offer strong employee incentives.
- *Beyond sales.* Saturn's salaried salespeople are called "sales consultants." The company hired sales consultants from outside the industry to minimize what it considered "bad habits."
- *Operating systems that deliver service.* There is great emphasis on leading edge and efficient service, customer, and dealer management processes and systems. The aim is to create an integrated and efficient supply chain management system for cars and parts, linking suppliers, the factory, and dealers.

Alternatively, suppliers can focus on improving their traditional sources of power. This is a typical but expensive and longer-term action. It also comes with increasingly dangerous caveats. A good product may not be enough to win or may not be sustainable. Similarly, bolstering the pull of a brand may well be economically unfeasible and a large installed base diminishes over time as product substitution nibbles away at it. Having a broad product line can be beneficial, but strong channel players will unbundle disadvantaged products.

The final option is to develop new channels and improve channel management including building extended enterprise capabilities to better serve end customers. These capabilities should aim to leverage scale and scope advantages. For example:

- Pooled inventories
- Vendor-managed inventories
- Category management and assortment management
- Display management
- Customer database marketing—detailed customer profiles
- Promotion management
- Customer profitability and market penetration systems
- Multiple channel management
- Order-to-delivery management

These various initiatives can be, in themselves, daunting. To give them coherence requires understanding of channel management as a process rather than an isolated initiative. The channel management process is made up of the five steps outlined in Section Two.

# Section Two

# The Channel Management Process

In this section we consider the channel management process as a whole. There are five basic steps:

1. *Understand customer buying and ownership needs and segments.*

The move from product-centered operations to effective channel management is substantial. Key to this is a clearer understanding of where in the supply chain customer value is added. The channel management process begins with identifying your end customers and gathering insights into your existing and potential relationship with them.

The aim is to deliver the right product–service bundle at the right price to the end customer. Understanding the customer is the only route to making this happen. Car companies, in particular, have found that a better understanding of the purchasing process enables them to identify new opportunities to add value. This has important implications for the balance of power between manufacturer and channel.

Customer insight is based on interaction with customers and potential customers and collection of customer-related data. Based on those insights, companies can then target particular groups of customers with the aim of delivering the service elements they value. As well as segmenting markets on a product basis, service-based differentiation requires that companies segment markets according to purchasing and ownership.

2.  *Develop new channel concepts to capture both customer and product life cycle value.*

The objective of segmentation is to enable a company to design different bundles of product attributes and associated services that will better match the needs and desires of different sets of consumers. To be profitable, these bundles must optimize the value delivered to each customer segment while being delivered economically. Deep customer insight can facilitate segments of one to be developed. In effect, channels are a means of mass service customization.

3.  *Pilot test to refine the economics and competitive positioning of the channel concepts—structures, services, and operational systems.*

Whether a channel is completely new or a carefully evolved network, the approach we recommend is to pilot test before plunging in. Piloting the new channel enables you to refine the economics and competitive positioning of the channel concepts—structures, services, and operational systems. Ideally, pilot tests are insulated, as much as possible, from the main business. This is primarily to minimize risk and refine the concepts before roll-out. They should be on the periphery of markets to minimize reactions from competitors until the business model you are seeking to develop is robust.

4.  *Rapidly roll out the concepts across segments and geographic territories.*

Once the channel offering has been refined, speed is of the essence. The changes should be deployed rapidly. When opening a new channel, being ahead of competitors can transform the market. This is especially the case when the end result is a personal, one-to-one relationship with the end consumer.

5.  *Study the results and adapt your channel.*

An effective channel provides two-way communication with the customer. This allows you to track customer requirements and revise the service offerings of the channels accordingly. Failure to do so will erode the channel offering over time. Channel management is a continuous process.

# Chapter 3
# Step One:
# Understand Customer Needs

> The price for each Saturn vehicle is determined by the separate decisions of three independent stakeholders: Saturn Corporation, the Retailer, and the Customer.
> —Saturn Pricing Principle

Customer care is often noticeable by its absence.

Research in the United Kingdom, for example, found that less than one-quarter of executives believed management hours spent with customers were important. At the same time, seven out of ten proclaimed that customer focus was the first or second priority for the organization's success.[1] Customer service is frequently misunderstood, misapplied, and mismanaged. At times it is off-puttingly excessive. At other times it is nonexistent. (It is as pointless to overserve as to underserve the customer. Overservice adds to cost without adding value.)

Undoubtedly, delivering service is demanding. "Where goods are first produced, then sold and finally consumed, services are first sold, then simultaneously produced and consumed. Since consumers need to be present during the production of many services, if only by telephone or electronic link, there is a closer interaction between buyer and seller," say the European academics Leslie de Chernatony and Francesca Riley. "The degree of interaction, and of consumer involvement, makes it more difficult to control service quality. Service organizations' brands are occasionally at the mercy of disgruntled, bad-tempered or simply inefficient customer-service staff. Furthermore, the customer experience may be affected by any number of unpredictable factors such as increased customer flow, poor branch environment or even customers' own moods. By effectively involving consumers in the production process, organizations are thrown into a high-risk but potentially high-gain situation day after day as customers experience the brand afresh."[2]

Similarly, failure to reinvent channels erodes their effectiveness. If you start a dialog with customers, you'd better make sure you listen to and act on what they tell you.

On top of—or perhaps because of—the complexity of providing excellent service, superficiality and lip service are endemic. But surprisingly little is said about the core problem many executives face: how do they ensure that their end customers receive the right service at the right price?

It sounds like a simple question to answer. The trouble is that manufacturing and service companies have little or limited control over the service the end consumer receives. At least half of all goods, and a significant portion of services, flow through distribution channels. Yet most of the extensive body of writing about customer care either addresses services provided directly to customers—by airlines, banks, hotels, and the like—or simply skirts the complication of dealing through intermediaries.

Over the years, many manufacturers have abdicated responsibility for customer relationships to retail outlets and distribution channels. Manufacturers have tended to think of retailers or distributors as their customers and have focused on maximizing sales to them. (This is called *loading the channel* and is achieved by, among other things, offering discounts for bulk purchasing. This strategy can create unintended effects, most notably big pileups of inventory in the channel, which lead to a stop-start pattern of orders, sales incentive payments, and, ultimately, to inefficient manufacturing or high product returns. Enlightened manufacturers have recognized this and are now beginning to structure incentives based on the channel's sales to the end user rather than purchases for inventory.)

Manufacturers have often preferred to maintain customer awareness of their brands through blanket advertising while handing over
day-to-day contact to dealerships and other channel players. This is a
dangerous move. It creates distance between the end user and the manufacturer. This is compounded when the manufacturer comes to regard
the channel player rather than the end user as the customer. In a variety of industries, a gap has developed between producers and end users.
The intermediary holds the reputation of the manufacturer in its hands.
If a customer buys a Volkswagen from a dealer, both the technical performance of the car and the service it receives make up the VW experience. Because the service element is the human element this is often
more important. The employee who books the car in for a service becomes the face of VW, yet is not employed by the company. VW has its
own savings bank. Why? To create opportunities to bond the customer
to the company and to the brand.

The new challenge for companies is to close this gap by thinking
beyond the channel. Product manufacturers should think not just about
their own economics in making and selling the product but also about
the economics of their distributors or retailers and even the economics
of the product's end user.

The reasons for this are most clearly illustrated through another example. Think about the value created—the money spent—through the
whole purchase and ownership cycle of a car. Looking at it the way
manufacturers usually do—50 percent to 60 percent of the value is in
the cost of parts it purchases from its suppliers, 20 to 30 percent goes
to labor, 10 to 15 percent to SG&A, and 0 to 5 percent to profit. In
other words, the value added by the manufacturer is 40 percent of the
wholesale price of the car.

But looking at it from the car buyer's point of view, another 30 percent or more is added after the factory gate and two to three times that
much in subsequent transactions carried out by the car owner without
any involvement on the part of the manufacturer—or even, necessarily,
the dealer (financing, insurance, maintenance, running costs).

Clearly from the car owner's point of view, the manufacturer is only
one of several players who influence the quality of the purchase and

ownership experience. The manufacturer has direct control over only a quarter of the total value delivered to the customer during the life of the car.

This is unhealthy for two reasons:

First, it means a missed opportunity. Clearly, if the manufacturer could get control of more of the value stream, it could potentially make more money. Moreover, by losing all contact with the customer at the point of sale, the manufacturer loses many of the potential benefits of customer relationships: the opportunity to learn from customer feedback, not to mention the inside track on selling the customer's next car. Exhibit 3.1 illustrates the influence of the channel on repeat purchase decisions.

Second, it can mean actual risk to the manufacturer's brand image. After all, it is the manufacturer's name on the car, even though there are many aspects of perceived quality over which it has little or no influence.

# The Search for Customer Insight

The essence of channel management is to reach the final customer in a way (through a channel) that adds value to the purchase and generates repeat business—that is, engenders loyalty. To do so requires companies to develop a deep understanding of customer behavior and preferences. Companies have to understand the whole range of consumer experience. We call this developing customer insight.

In the past, companies have tended to base decisions on what customers do rather than why they do it. Channel management requires digging deeper so as to understand what makes customers tick: what they like and don't like about their experiences as customers. To gather this information and use it effectively requires companies to behave in new ways.

Customer insight, then, is a combination of skills, tangible tools, processes, and structures, embedded in a "consumer culture" and founded on how the company chooses to compete. Such insight is characteristic of companies that shape the future by acting faster today. It is transforming them, as illustrated in Exhibit 3.2.

# Exhibit 3.1    Channel Power: Effects of Satisfaction with Dealer

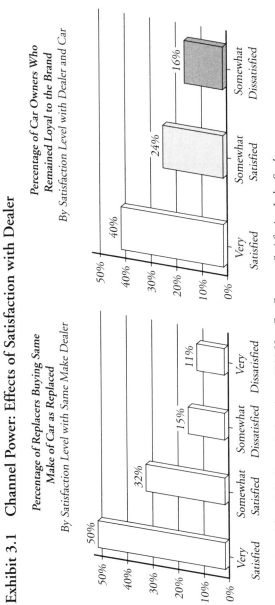

Percentage of Replacers Buying Same
Make of Car as Replaced
By Satisfaction Level with Same Make Dealer

Percentage of Car Owners Who
Remained Loyal to the Brand
By Satisfaction Level with Dealer and Car

*Source:* Adapted from J. D. Power & Associates. *1993 New Car Customer Satisfaction Index Study.*

**Exhibit 3.2 Changes in Insightful Companies**

|  | *From* | *To* |
|---|---|---|
| Scope | • Consumer decisions | • Consumer experience |
| Boundaries | • Product markets | • Consumer value |
| Outlook | • Predict the future | • Understand the "here and now" |
| Focus | • Trends | • Opportunities |
| Research | • Support decisions | • Build insight |
| Market Research | • Owning information | • Owning processes |
| Market Testing | • Demonstration | • Experimentation |

While many claim to be driven by the customer, few companies are able to develop true customer insight, and even fewer are able to turn insight into action. (As a host of recent books and articles proclaim, effective knowledge management is all about turning what you know into competitive advantage.) Those companies that do so are characterized by four elements:

• External Interface
  Bring customer understanding into the organization.
  Take management out into the customer environment.
• Internal Processes
  Build information into management insight and company knowledge.
  Share customer understanding across the whole organization.
• Organization and Culture
  Optimize insight gathering and dissemination.
  Motivate and reward to create consumer focus.
  Provide a supporting infrastructure—training, recruitment, performance measurement.
• Insightful Action
  Make customer insight the starting point of core processes.
  Integrate insight into systems and process infrastructure.

The reality is that leading companies demonstrate a customer-focused culture at all levels. They change continually—and they change top-down, outside-in, inside-out—and they build formal processes to create and sustain the culture. The end result is the virtuous circle shown in Exhibit 3.3. Consumer insight allows them to generate ideas in keeping with the needs, concerns, and aspirations of customers—and these ideas can then be developed, marketed, and assessed to feed into new consumer insights.

Customer insight is based, fundamentally, on getting close to customers. Historically information came through a narrow pipe. Now

**Exhibit 3.3   Consumer Insight Virtuous Circle**

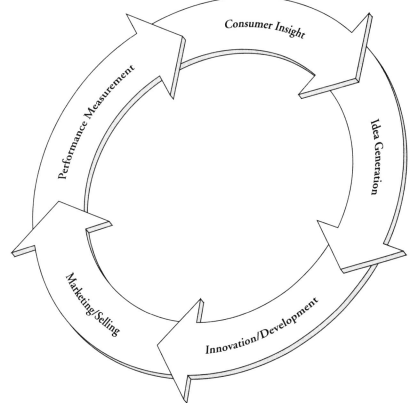

companies receive broadband information through multiple sources—consumer panels, loyalty programs, sponsored events. (The possibilities are mapped out in Exhibit 3.4.) With technological improvements offering more accessible information, companies have many opportunities to leverage end customer knowledge. Some of those messages will be contradictory, but no one said this was going to be easy.

Opening windows to consumers allows a company to develop a deeper understanding of the whole consumer experience, based on the synthesis of hard and soft data from many sources. Some windows are spontaneous, some interactive, and others based on systematic monitoring. Formal processes distribute information and insight as broadly as possible throughout the organization, integrating the consumer into the way the company does business.

Distribution is no longer on a "need to know" basis. Senior and nonmarketing management receive regular updates. Organizations make greater use of electronic ways of distributing information. Insight is built by sharing new types of information in more involving, often informal ways. This requires roles to be changed.

The role of market research, for example, becomes dissemination of consumer *information* rather than just data. It becomes one of many consumer hubs that facilitate access to rather than ownership of the consumer. Ultimately, information flow needs to ensure that the consumer:

- Shapes management's agenda
- Feeds its dialogue
- Motivates the organization

# Understanding Data

To understand your customers, you must collect, understand, and assimilate information and data on them.

At Bank of America, managers have access to the company's customer database. Using an individual customer's profile and behaviors

**Exhibit 3.4   Listening to the Customer**

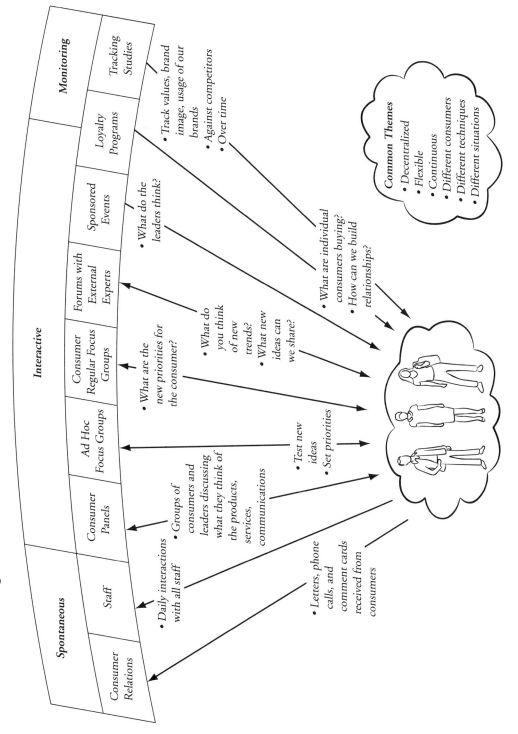

*Source:* Interview data

## Moments of Truth

One way to look at building an understanding of customer needs is in terms of what Jan Carlzon, former head of SAS, called *moments of truth*—the sequence of critical transactions across each stage of the ownership or use cycle.

- Initial contact
- First use
- Problem solving
- Ongoing support
- Further purchases
- Recommendations to others

Evaluating the degree to which satisfaction and value are affected at these different points in the cycle, and how they vary by customer type, can be the key to understanding customer behavior.

An interesting example of a moments-of-truth analysis is in the cellular phone service industry, where most consumers have only one interaction with a channel, at the time of the original sale. In the United States, high satisfaction with this initial sales experience is critically important. It translates into a longer association with the service provider (that is, less customer churn), which is the primary determinant of customer profitability. The satisfaction level is based on how well the sales channel explains features and service charges and sets up the consumer with proper expectations.

This insight cannot be overly broadly applied, however. A car manufacturer found that an important source of customer dissatisfaction with the buying process could be overcome by having dealer sales personnel carefully explain operating and instrument display functions. Unfortunately, the manufacturer failed to realize that while some customers were pleased with this service, others were put off by having to sit through a mandated demonstration session that they viewed as bothersome and perfunctory. The mistake was to treat all customers alike. Such standardized customer service policies are endemic in automotive and other retailing industries. Simply asking the purchaser whether a demonstration would add value could have eliminated the irritation factor.

## Channel Champions: Armstrong's World

Armstrong World Industries recognized that home centers, its key retailers, were an emerging and rapidly growing channel. The growth within the segment was tremendous. But as the opportunity ripened, Armstrong wasn't sure how to address it. Analysis of the U.S. home center market in 1996 showed outstanding opportunities for sales. The entire home improvement retail channel was worth about $140 billion. Continuing annual growth of over 5 percent was anticipated. The three top players—Home Depot, Lowe's, and Menard's—were expected to continue to gain share at the expense of other home centers and grow at over 20 percent annually, going from 25 percent to 40 percent of the home improvement market. It was expected that the total number of "big box" stores would grow to close to 2,700 in five years, a 66 percent increase over 1995.[3]

| COMPANY | Armstrong World Industries, Inc. | |
|---|---|---|
| ADDRESS | 2500 Columbia Avenue, P.O. Box 3001, Lancaster PA 17604 USA<br>Phone: 717–397–0611<br><br>URL: http://www.armstrong.com | |
| BUSINESS | Home improvement products | |
| STATISTICS | Employees | 1998   18,900 |
| | Annual sales (mil) | 1998   $2,746 |
| | Annual results (mil) | 1998   $221 (excluding one-time charges) |
| | Other facts | A leader in residential and commercial flooring, flooring installation and maintenance products, acoustical ceiling and wall products, and cabinets |

Channel Champions: Armstrong's World (continued)

As competition heated up, Armstrong thought it was enough to lower prices. It did not believe that the home center market would value service. But further analysis found that service was a significant differentiator. Accordingly, Armstrong determined that aggressive efforts to address this channel were necessary.

Armstrong wanted to create a strategy to aggressively manage and serve its largest clients. Customers identified several key areas and the relevant requirements necessary to succeed within that area. Within sales, customers wanted a supplier with one face, full and direct responsibility and authority, incentives aligned to account performance, and empowered decision makers. Within the in-store service area they wanted training, new store sets, major resets, merchandising and replenishment assistance, and claims and problem-solving assistance. Logistically they were looking for a 100 percent fill rate with no stock outs, high inventory turns, efficient services (at low cost), and a seven-day maximum delivery cycle. As far as category management, customers were looking for flexible and customized programs, exclusive products, and reliable information. Transactionally they wanted a single point of contact, electronic processing and exchange of information, accurate and timely invoicing, and reliable delivery of information.

In response, Armstrong developed capabilities to provide one face to the customer. It worked on two specific things: managing inventory at the site (cleaning up the storage of broken tiles, rotating stock, training people) and providing computer tools using point of sale (POS) data. As a result inventory turns went up sharply.[4]

In an attempt to provide top-quality services to its large and growing national accounts, Armstrong introduced the Corporate Retail Accounts (CRA) division in April 1994. This reflected Armstrong's determination to increase market share in all its businesses by creating new capabilities and upgrading services that had been provided by the company's national accounts sales organization for many years. CRA is a purely market-centered organization, focused not on products or manufacturing processes but on the needs of a specific group of customers.

CRA customers are large, multilocation retailers who sell multiple corporate products in the North American residential and commercial markets. Sales to this group of customers reached a new annual record in 1994. In fact, sales for each successive month in 1994 established a new monthly record. The CRA marketing strategy is aimed at becoming its customers' supplier of choice for these and any other product categories in the Armstrong corporate offering. The key to achieving that position is the division's development of a superior value proposition for its customers—based not only on products but also on brand strategies, merchandising and in-store service, information support, and logistics systems. In short, CRA is reaching its own sales and income objectives by maximizing the sales and income its customers realize. The early goal of CRA was to provide the big box retailers (the focus of CRA and the segment that had been growing at double-digit rates and accounting for fully 12 percent of Armstrong's sales) top-quality, customized service.

A major aim was to improve logistical cost effectiveness. In order to do so, fifteen independent regional distribution centers were planned to serve these customers. These centers provided customers with centralized order management and coordinated shipments. Armstrong foresaw cost savings through logistics improvement—especially full truckload deliveries and reduced administrative paperwork associated with order fulfillment.

Another goal of CRA was to improve retailer gross margin return on investment. One of the primary functions of the group was to meet the demanding service requirements of giant retailers such as Home Depot and Lowe's. Customized support took the form of assisting with merchandising and merchandise displays, store employee training, and information and logistics systems support.

Armstrong's "total category management" approach entailed differentiated programs for big box retailers, so they were provided with the products and services that drive value for their customers. Armstrong worked with customers to determine their needs and identify the right products from among its flooring, ceiling, installation, and insulation offerings. It also began to advise on the proper product mix and merchandising, provide in-store training, and structure the ordering and billing processes to fit each retailer's needs. Technological investments improved its processes by generating fact-based, customer-specific information, allowing Armstrong to be more responsive

Channel Champions: Armstrong's World (continued)

to its customers' requirements. Key elements included coordinating multiproduct shipments, scheduling weekly deliveries, and simplifying the supply processes.

Throughout 1996, the division made numerous strides in enhancing these capabilities, all of which helped grow its business by 17 percent. Commercial and residential tile product sales increased by 31 percent and 19 percent respectively, due in part to the segmentation strategy started in late 1995, which provided exclusive products and sub-brands to specific retailers.

By the end of 1996, the CRA big box customer base included 1,600 retail stores that purchase many of Armstrong's flooring, ceiling and grid, installation, and insulation products. Armstrong expected that base to grow to approximately 2,300 stores by the year 2000 through existing and new customers.

Sales to CRA customers in 1994 established new records in every corporate product category. The CRA program generated nearly $330 million in sales, or 12 percent of total company sales, with less than $50 million in nonmanufacturing expenses. CRA sales increased over 20 percent in 1995, well above the company's overall sales growth of about 4 percent, and accounted for 18 percent to 20 percent of the company's total floor coverings and building products sales.

As of December 1996, Armstrong stated that the CRA program was a success. The program had become an integral part of the company's business. Armstrong sales to the big box retailers were fully 16 percent of its total sales in 1996 and were up 17 percent from 1995 to become the company's fastest-growing segment.

A solid gain in this business was especially noteworthy in 1995, a year in which many suppliers to that channel suffered

(responses to previous marketing offers), managers can identify products the customer is likely to want and offer them on the spot, before the customer leaves the bank.

At British Airways, the airline has software that allows it to give first class, business class, and frequent flyers all their flying preferences—everything from drinks to newspapers and movies—without the passenger's having to ask.

eroding sales because of an inventory correction that was under way. Sales to Corporate Retail Accounts advanced by 18 percent in 1996, and rose even more quickly in early 1997. For 1998, Armstrong reported an increase in receivables of $35.9 million and stated that one of the primary reasons for the increase was a high level of billings related to CRA.

*Channels by Armstrong*

- *Develop information systems.* By developing systems to closely monitor its customers' sales of individual products in all corporate categories, CRA provided Armstrong and subsidiary business unit teams with fact-based information and market data to identify opportunities and customer requirements, guide new product development, and shorten cycle times. With its market-centered sales and service organization and its specialized information and distribution systems, CRA is equipped to generate immediate sales volume for new products—including product categories that are totally new to Armstrong.
- *Change with the business.* One of the keys to Armstrong's fundamental resurgence has been its successful adjustment to the substantial shift that has developed in distribution patterns for building materials. Large home center chains are gradually supplanting traditional wholesalers, lumberyards, and specialty distributors. Armstrong's CRA operation, which provides an integrated package of products and services to these big box retailers, has been one of the company's fastest-growing units. Fifteen regional distribution centers serve these customers.

Analyzing detailed customer data allows companies to more cost-effectively and efficiently target specific new customers. "Our success will depend on understanding exactly what the customer wants," says Malcolm McDonald, president and CEO of Signet Bank.

First, there is the question of costs. Using data effectively can help reduce costs. Capital One Financial evaluated its customers' behavior patterns and applied predictive models. It saved $280 million. With enough data, a company can locate customers more effectively by targeting potential customers already predisposed to purchase the product. Data collection and analysis also helps companies serve customers faster with fewer transactions, which lowers costs and cycle times.

If you know your audience, you can target it in a much more effective way than by pursuing mass marketing. Once you separate profitable customers from unprofitable customers, activities can be focused accordingly.

Pizza Hut found that frequent users have a value of $600 per year and now focuses its attentions on attracting and retaining these consumers. Pitney Bowes found that two-thirds of its business came from less than 10 percent of its customers. Even McDonald's has its Super Heavy Users—SHUs for short.

Dell uses data to identify unprofitable customers that should be dropped from its direct mail list. This saved $4 million in a single year. MBNA applies models that use customer buying habits and trends to identify which customers will be profitable. Nonprofitable ones are removed from the marketing efforts and more extensive promotions and campaigns are targeted at profitable customers. MBNA increased its profits sixteenfold by reducing its attrition rate to half the industry average and by identifying customers likely to be profitable.

The more you know about customer behavior patterns, the more responsive you can be to nuances in consumer behavior and preferences. Predictive modeling allows you to predict consumer behavior and to try to meet trends as they occur. This also saves money. USAA emphasizes building lifelong relationships. This enables it to find new customers with little effort. There is no need for expensive aggressive marketing when you know what is going on in the lives of your potential customers. The fifteen-year-old daughter of a USAA customer will receive information about learning to drive just as she is old enough to take Driver's Education.

Sears, for example, found that women shopped in its stores more often than men. It was able to adjust its marketing to speak more directly to women through "The softer side of Sears" campaign. Sears also uses customer buying behavior to track all sales and to determine which customers are buying frequently and which are not. The company then promotes its offerings based on the frequency level of purchases. Sears uses data to ensure that it adjusts its ranges in line with customer needs. By using data to track life events, the company can observe trends in purchasing habits.

You have a head start when you keep careful track of customer data. Among other things, this understanding helps you attract new customers that don't currently buy any product or service. Effectively, you can preempt the decision process and build aspirations prior to the purchase. Caterpillar developed a model that allowed it to use its databases of buying habits, needs, and other relevant information to determine which noncustomers were likely to become customers.

And armed with the right data you can effectively target the customers of competitors. Jaguar sends extravagant mailings to people who own or lease competitive models, offering such premiums as Montblanc pens to encourage test drives.

The major use of data is to create closer and longer relationships with existing customers. Studies have shown that a 2 percent cut in attrition rates has the same bottom-line effect as a 10 percent cut in costs. This leads to increased revenue with lower costs. This virtuous arrangement has a number of elements:

• *By knowing each customer well, companies are able to predict what additional products the customer may need or desire.* 1–800-Flowers collects information about special dates—such as birthdays and anniversaries—for its customers. As those dates approach, it sends reminders, suggesting that it's time to send some flowers or one of the company's other products. Cross-selling—through complementary or supplementary products—becomes far easier. United Audio developed its "purchase after purchase" campaign. This uses information based on customer sales to target customers that may be interested in complementary products to those already acquired.

Improved understanding of customer needs increases the consistency and quality of service. Norwegian Cruise Lines no longer uses mass mailings; it creates a specific cruise experience based on customer groups with similar profiles.

Customer information is a proprietary asset that can be turned into a competitive advantage that could take months or even years to imitate.

Meanwhile, building customer loyalty may make customers feel as though they need your product. This is encouraged through reminders about the product, continual personal contact, special treatment, and assistance with services related to the product sold. Nordstrom sales clerks make notes of "good" customer selections. When a customer's preferred item comes in, the sales clerk will personally call to inform the customer of the new item's arrival.

Knowing what the customer needs and adjusting your offerings accordingly can result in increased visits to your store—encouraged by increased promotions, customized offers, and frequent user programs. MCI examined patterns in its customer database and found that substantial numbers of households regularly placed long distance calls to a maximum of twelve households. In response, it created its "Friends and Family" program.

You don't have to be a multinational giant to get fantastic results from data-inspired promotions. A twelve-restaurant chain with 450,000 guests registered as part of its birthday club sent every guest a mailing. This generated more than 400,000 total guest visits and in excess of $3.1 million in sales.

Similarly, a seven-restaurant chain mailed 40,471 birthday cards, received 34,832 guest visits, 13,071 redemptions, and $288,000 in sales. Another holiday time special offer generated a further 9,391 visits and $76,000 in sales.

◆ ◆ ◆

The next question is what do companies actually do to collect data? They do so in a million different ways. Many use data to cost-effectively target specific new customers:

- Bank of America assesses each of its 75 million customers' monthly spending habits and responses to previous promotional offers to determine whether it is worth continuing marketing efforts and, if so, what specific offers would be appropriate and when they should be targeted at a particular individual.

- US West, the telecom company, determines how much of a customer's telecom budget it is already getting, then determines whether it is worth continuing marketing efforts.
- 3Com uses a mass mailer to collect information about customer needs and computer usage habits. As a result, target promotions are mailed to high-quality leads.
- Reader's Digest obtains initial customer information from electoral registers and from data-gathering companies. Affluent potential customers are then bombarded with mailings.
- American Express uses buying behavior data to determine customers' preferences. Based on those preferences, it attaches targeted promotions to the billing statements. It can also produce the aggregated spending activities of any cardholder. This helps retailers pinpoint which customers use their Amex cards the most and at which times there are more shoppers.

The goal of all this data collection and analysis is to try to build customer relationships that will result in increased revenue with lower costs. In short, the aim is to build a lifelong relationship with the customer, in order to most effectively and efficiently provide that customer with the highest-quality products and services possible.

## Understanding Loyalty

Armed with customer insight and based on data about consumer preferences and behavior, it is advisable to pause for breath and contemplate the meaning of loyalty.

In business, loyalty is increasingly elusive. Service differentiates. Excellent service is often built on simple foundations, delivering the relatively small number of things customers want and value. The trouble is that we live in an age of increasing customer choice, customer power, and customer segment fragmentation. Consumers are more fickle than ever before. Product loyalty no longer holds sway. People who are apparently happy with the product can switch. Indeed, the term loyalty is often a misnomer—on average the most frequent business travelers are "loyal" to three different frequent-flyer schemes. And this pattern is repeated across products as diverse as gas retailing and coffee. "Exclusive loyalty is the exception not the norm. The reasons for this are prosaic. In the case of airlines, a particular carrier may not have the desired route available. For grocery goods a customer's favorite brand may not be in stock or not prominently displayed; or perhaps the customer wanted a change or there may have been a special promotion," observes Mark Uncles of the University of Western Australia.[5]

The basis for loyalty is not necessarily purely economic. There is more to loyalty and more to business success than simply getting people to repurchase your product. People repurchase some public utilities' services every month but remain steadfastly dissatisfied. Likewise, people may upgrade to every new release of Windows even though they appear to have a limited bond with Microsoft.

We believe there is a loyalty continuum measured on one axis by price premium (or gross margin) and on the other axis by loyalty, as shown in Exhibit 3.5.

The loyalty axis begins with economic loyalty. Economic loyalty is, in practice, usually purchased as a discount price; indeed, it is hardly loyalty at all. Consumers will depart with a minimum of fuss. This can be seen in commodity purchases—any iceberg lettuce or any paper clip will do—and where there are a limited number of offerings to be considered—such as whether to buy from KFC or Boston Market, Bumble Bee or Chicken of the Sea.

Moving up the scale there is an increasing degree of loyalty as economic factors become mixed with emotional ones. This stage has strong psychographic drivers—such as family, belonging, and independence—and includes products such as Apple Computers, Michelin, Marlboro, and Coke.

Finally, there is the primarily emotional end of the continuum where there is absolute loyalty. These might include political causes, religion, and family. There is a sense of belonging. There is a sense that you have exceeded customer expectations, gone out of your way to meet their needs. Here there is a real relationship and studies have shown that

**Exhibit 3.5    Price versus Loyalty**

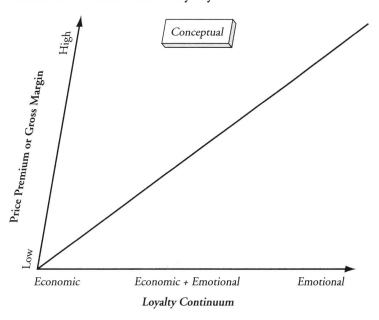

customers with more relationships with a particular company are less likely to move to the competition.

The price premium increases as you move to the right of the continuum, until eventually you end up paying for the right to be loyal—for example, because of love for your country or family.

Clearly, this is another nail in the coffin of product-based differentiation. Incremental product and image superiority alone cannot warrant a sustained price premium of 25 percent and up. The typical logic behind a purchase used to be that a consumer bought a product because it was a little better than competing products. It didn't have to be a great deal better. It was a little better and did the job for which it was intended. The underlying logic was that the consumer didn't have to worry or think about the purchase decision. The product was better. Period.

In many cases what then happened was that there was a flurry of promotions. Consumers began to think about the purchase decision.

This resulted in a fairly rational purchase decision process and eventually led to lower price premiums. The entire process failed to engender emotional commitment and was caught in a downward spiral.

Of course, some still believe that if your product is superior, you engender loyalty. The reality is that while it is easier to get loyalty if you offer a superior product, it is difficult to create and maintain truly superior products—it demands hefty R&D investments and, as we have seen, copycats are sure to follow. Also, product superiority must be kept simple enough so that it can be communicated to consumers. At the same time, it must be reflected in useful—value-adding—features: it must *feel* superior.

The reality is that relationships only prosper if there is an emotional bond. Consumers may repurchase your product. They may even prefer it in comparison to your competitors' products, but are they in love with your brand? Do they care about the relationship they have with you?

While this is an odd question, it is likely to become an increasingly important one. You will need an emotional bond because, with the advent of power retailing and now e-commerce, search costs are asymptotic to zero in many categories. Reassurance has gone. Witness the growth in private label merchandise and the number of consumers who feel it's as good as the national brands.

Another way of looking at the loyalty continuum is to see it as a hierarchy of customer relationships similar to Abraham Maslow's hierarchy of needs. Maslow's hierarchy, first published in 1943, argued that there was an ascending scale of needs that must be addressed if people are to be motivated. The hierarchy parallels the human life cycle. First are the fundamental physiological needs of warmth, shelter, and food. Once basic physiological needs are met, others emerge. Next on the hierarchy are social (or love) needs, and ego (or self-esteem) needs. Ultimately, as a person moves up the scale, with each need being satisfied comes what Maslow labeled "self-actualization" and individuals achieve their own personal potential. "A musician must make music, an artist must paint, a poet must write, if he is to be ultimately at peace with himself. What a man be, he must be," said Maslow.

We believe there are four rungs to the ladder of loyalty, illustrated in Exhibit 3.6.

**Exhibit 3.6   Ladder of Loyalty**

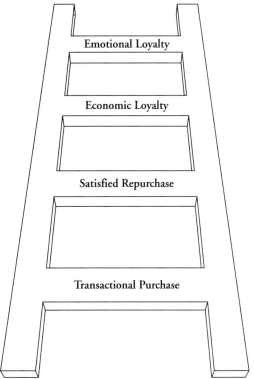

- *First Rung: Transactional Purchase*

At this stage, there's no loyalty in the strict sense of the word. Consumers evaluate every purchase and make a decision as to what they buy. This may—or may not—lead to repurchase. This depends on issues such as pricing. Repurchase in this context is ephemeral in nature. For some types of products it can be powerful for long periods of time, but it's naturally assailable.

- *Second Rung: Satisfied Repurchase*

Consumers make their purchase decision based on a positive experience—"I liked it the last time"—or the expectation of a positive experience created by word of mouth (more powerful) or advertising (less powerful). Experience goods, such as most services (from doctors to consultants), are particularly apt to fall into this category.

While this step is more powerful than transactional repurchase, satisfied repurchases are still tenuous. One bad experience can terminate the relationship. Similarly, a competitor's innovation (whether real or a gimmick) or promotion can also alter the relationship.

- *Third Rung: Economic Loyalty*

Here we enter the true realm of loyalty—continued positive experience narrows the consideration set: it's not that search costs are high, it's that the expected benefit from the search is low. Emotional loyalty acts as a buffer against negative experiences, which can be attributed to chance, and also against innovation—with economic loyalty, it's OK to be a fast follower sometimes (unless innovation is at the core of the value).

Research shows that pioneering brands in a category have higher loyalty with consumers than later copies. One interpretation is that being first allows consumers to build economic loyalty to the product. Economic loyalty can be seen with McDonald's in the young families segment of the fast-food market, and in the battle between Reebok and Nike.

- *Highest Rung: Emotional Loyalty*

Emotional loyalty is an affective bond with the brand. In Maslow's terminology, it is a means of self-actualization. It is a higher level of satisfaction, one that satisfies an emotional need. Brands that engender emotional loyalty can evolve beyond the specific field to be aspirational in nature. And the beauty is that no category is exempt. Exhibit 3.7 illustrates the variety of businesses that have found it possible to establish an emotional bond with their customers.

## Climbing the Loyalty Ladder

Despite extensive research in academia and practitioner circles, we still don't know enough about how affective bonds are formed between people in general, much less vis-à-vis a commercial brand. But, we do know that they are real. We are beginning to draw from other disciplines (psychology, sociology, communication, and political science) to figure out how to foster them and manage them.

**Exhibit 3.7   Examples of Emotional Loyalty to Brands**

| Brand | Description and Insight |
| --- | --- |
| Michelin | • Your safety versus your kids' safety<br>• Innovations as the source of economic loyalty |
| Volvo | • Family safety; also reliability |
| McDonald's | • U.S.: Economic loyalty with kids and traveling adults<br>• International: A piece of Americana |
| Snap-on | • Reliable and knowledgeable vendor; high-quality product |
| Marlboro | • American idealism; the great outdoors |

However, some general rules seem to apply:

- You cannot achieve emotional loyalty without having climbed the other rungs of the loyalty ladder.
- You must understand the aspirations and motivations of the customer—and appeal to the "higher you."
- You must manage all the points of contact with the emotionally loyal consumer.
- Emotionally loyal consumers have higher expectations—they cannot be defrauded. It is critical to understand and manage the emotionally loyal constituency—think politics, not marketing.

While generating emotional loyalty may be expensive, it's also worth it—these are probably the least price-sensitive segments. The rational (mostly product price-related) side tends to increase the overall percentage of total purchase occasions, but the emotional side tends to exact higher price premiums. Branded products extract a price premium of around 25 percent; products that cannot add the emotional element to the purchase exact lower margins (typically by around 15 to 20 percentage points lower).

## Becoming Emotional

While not all the elements are fully understood, companies need to start assessing where they are on the loyalty ladder—and experimenting with different ways to climb the ladder.

What should companies do? They need to understand the mechanics of loyalty and the loyalty ladder. As an example, think of the purchasing process that lies behind buying tires. This purchase has an emotional element. Michelin has high brand loyalty intensity thanks to its emotionally appealing identification with babies and safety. Prior to Michelin's "baby" marketing, no one thought of a tire as an emotional purchase.

The strength of such emotional appeal is that, in some instances, consumers buy the product even when it is inferior. When Harley-Davidson had quality problems, consumers remained loyal because of the emotional appeal. Now that quality has improved drastically Harley has both good product attributes and a strong emotional appeal, which has resulted in tremendous intensity of loyalty.

Harley, like many others, also makes use of the emotional appeal to "buy American." Buy American is raw emotion. It works, but only to a point. The general rule is that emotional strings need to be tugged more subtly and indirectly. "Like A Rock" from Chevrolet is an example of where it works. The message is, "I'm struggling a little, but I'm taking care of my family, working hard, and we'll make it through this."

The message is that truly differentiated appeal requires the noneconomic (emotional) side to reinforce product attributes. If it is done right, the image side of the brand can be a stronger driver than the product side. While the product side can be duplicated, it is very hard to compete with or copy the emotional side. In combination, product and emotional appeal raise the price premium and the percentage of repurchase increases.

## Brands for Loyalty

In the quest for loyalty, channels are increasingly reconstituted as brands. At the same time, brands have been reconstituted as emotional weapons. Brands have moved beyond products. Exhibit 3.8 gives a stark example

Exhibit 3.8    What Makes Customers Loyal

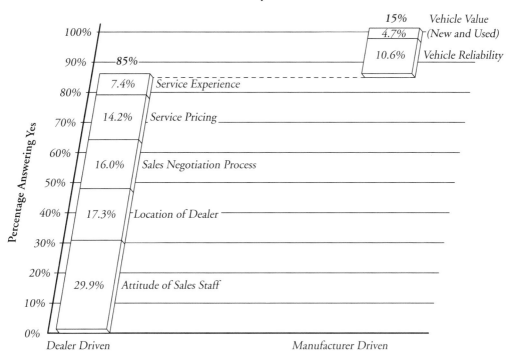

*Source:* R.L. Polk 1997 Manufacturers Loyalty Survey

of the decreasing impact of the product—in automobile sales, regard for the vehicle itself accounts for only about 15 percent of the customer's repurchase decision.

The traditional view of what constitutes a brand is summed up by marketing guru Philip Kotler in his classic textbook *Marketing Management.* Kotler writes: "[A brand name is] a name, term, sign, symbol or design, or a combination of these, which is intended to identify the goods or services of one group of sellers and differentiate them from those of competitors."

The trouble with older definitions of brands is that they remain preoccupied with the physical product. The product stands alone; the brand exists within corporate ether. The product comes first and the brand does little more than make it clear which company made the product and where. However, although the Saturn automobile may be the product, the Saturn brand is much more.

A more recent definition comes from Richard Koch in his book *The Dictionary of Financial Management.* Koch defines a brand as: "A visual design and/or name that is given to a product or service by an organization in order to differentiate it from competing products and which assures consumers that the product will be of high and consistent quality." Reflecting the emphasis of our times, Koch stresses differentiation—making your product or service different (or seem to be different)—and achieving consistent quality. For example, Club Med is a brand for all the destinations it presents. People decide to go to Club Med knowing it will have a certain format and a certain type of service, and then pick a destination.

"The point of brands is, and always has been, to provide information. The form of that information varies from market to market, and from time to time. Some products make a visible statement about their users' style, modernity or wealth—examples include clothes, cars and accessories. Others purport to convey reliability, say, or familiarity, or something else. Whatever the information, however, the right question to ask is this: Does the buyer still need or want it?" acutely observed an editorial in the *Economist.*[6] From being product-centered, brands are now service-oriented.

Brands come in a small number of basic forms:

• *Manufacturer's brands.* This is supposedly self-evident, such as Coke or Tide or Mercedes-Benz. But there are fewer and fewer examples of manufacturers' brands that have retained their value to end consumers over a long period of time.

• *Channels as brands.* Partly because of the increasing importance of channel-delivered value, channels—such as a retail chain like Wal-Mart—are increasingly able to create their own brands, which can become more powerful with end consumers than the product manufacturers' brands. If we visit Home Depot we go to buy any given category, for selection and price, as opposed to a given brand. Similarly, Saturn is really the branding of the channel more than the car.

Channel branding increases the channel's importance and power, enabling it to control more of the value in the value chain. If a manufacturer with an independent channel is affected by this trend and does nothing about it, it will find its margins eroded (at best) and may even lose touch with its end users entirely.

• *Brands within channels.* Suppliers often provide goods and services explicitly for a distribution channel—private label is an example of a channel brand. Typically, these are heavily advertised but are used by retailers to make more money—consumers come into a store looking for heavily advertised brands and are steered toward other brands on which the retailer makes a bigger margin. Famous examples of private label brands include Kenmore (appliances) and Craftsman (tools), sold only at Sears retail outlets.

Ceding ownership of the customer relationship to the channel is commonly a key component of supplier brand erosion. Thus, to retain and enhance brand value, suppliers must ensure that the desired service elements are provided adequately and consistently and that the marketing mix reinforces the service image.

# Segmentation by Purchasing

If you possess customer insights built on exhaustive data and interaction and you understand the nature of loyalty and the role of brands, you can move on to look at how best to target particular segments of the market.

Both products and services can be used to target segments. Products target the features and service targets the overall interaction. We suggest two additional segmentation dimensions (in addition to traditional product-based dimensions):

First, there is segmentation based on the purchasing process.

How do people want to buy something? In the car market, for example, distribution channels have slowly evolved in large part due to regulations and high costs. New channels are now being rapidly developed as product segmentation gives way to purchase segmentation.

The American auto industry is facing a barrage of new channel formats that fulfill various elements of the traditional dealer role in selling new cars. There are information exchanges on the Internet; there are

## Brand the Gap

The Gap's Christmas 1996 slogan was "Every color—only Gap"—the contemporary antithesis of Henry Ford's "Any color you like as long as it's black." Founded in 1969, for a number of years the retail chain was content to sell Levi's jeans and identify itself with the lowercase "gap" logo. In the 1970s and early 1980s, the enclosed mall shopping concept was really taking off and creating a recognizable retail outlet was a sensible strategy. But as the look of clothes retailing changed in the 1980s, Gap began to seem dated. Other retail stores had copied the Gap formula, using similar store design and selling look-alike products. Multicolored T-shirts and sweatshirts were piled high in many clothes stores that replicated the Gap feel and atmosphere. The original had to do something to preserve its position.

CEO Millard "Mickey" Drexler realized it was time for the Gap to stop thinking of itself as a retailer and start thinking like a brand. The result is the creation of one of the star brands of recent years.

In 1983, the company changed its logo to long, clean-limbed uppercase letters to become The GAP. By 1991, it had reinvented itself, dropping the Levi's line altogether. But The GAP stores are only one part of the story. In the United States, the company also revitalized Banana Republic—acquired in 1983, tired by the 1990s, since rejuvenated. Gap also introduced Old Navy Clothing stores in 1994, with a warehouse feel to the outlets.

In effect, the company fashioned three distinctive channels targeted at different market segments. At the top end, there is Banana Republic; at the lower end, Old Navy; and occupying the upper-middle ground, the Gap brand. Key to the brand offering in all three cases is freshness. The company is constantly introducing new colors and rotating its offerings to ensure that whatever the season or the latest fashion, you can walk into its stores and find something that is entirely contemporary.

The company has successfully integrated brand name identification supported by marketing and advertising into its merchandising operation. The clean, uncluttered look that is the hallmark of the Gap brand image works just as well across age groups. With more than a thousand stores in the United States, Canada, France, Germany, Japan, and the United Kingdom—plus over 550 GapKids and BabyGaps outlets—creatively, all the Gap branding has the same feel and stands for the same simple clothes designs.

| COMPANY | The Gap, Inc. | |
|---|---|---|
| ADDRESS | One Harrison Street, San Francisco CA 94105 USA<br>Phone: 650–952–4400   Fax: 650–427–2795<br><br>URL: http://www.gap.com | |
| BUSINESS | Specialty retail—clothing | |
| STATISTICS | Employees | 1998    81,000 |
| | Annual sales (mil) | 1998    $6,507 |
| | Annual results (mil) | 1998    $533 |
| | Other facts | Roughly 2,300 casual clothing stores in Canada, France, Germany, Japan, the United Kingdom, and the United States |

Drexler's insight proved prescient. Since 1994, when some commentators were writing the company off as a "mature business," sales have skyrocketed. "They made their name into a brand," notes one leading retailing analyst. "They are one of the few retailers who have that luxury."[7] In this case, the channel brands overwhelmingly dominated and subsumed the previous product brands (such as Levi's) sold through its outlets. The Gap is able to produce and sell its own-label products, which is a much more profitable proposition than selling others' branded products.

Once bitten by the branding bug, Drexler is said to have immersed himself in information about the world's leading brands, especially Coca-Cola. It is no coincidence that Sergio Zyman, a senior marketing executive from Coca-Cola, was invited to join the Gap board of directors.

The company is taking no chances. It is pouring advertising money into its brand strategy like gasoline to keep the flames high. In 1996, the company spent around $100 million; in 1997, it spent $150 million.

## Brand the Gap (continued)

In 1995, recognizing the strength of its brand appeal, the Gap added a line of personal care products packaged with an upbeat stainless steel look that complemented the brand aesthetics and the no-nonsense feel of its stores.

The new product line radiated quality, but affordable quality. It was designer design—without designer prices.

In recent years, too, the company has shown a willingness to move with the times, extending its brand to new channel formats such as Internet shopping. Above all it is easy shopping. Stores offer easy access and garments are color coordinated for customers. The company's first major TV advertising campaign in twelve years was kicked off by rap artist LL Cool J. The rap? "How easy is this?"

buying clubs that act as sales intermediaries and on-line purveyors of financing options; there are auto malls and megadealers. More than ever before, manufacturers and dealers are being pressed to evaluate how best to serve the very different needs of different customers. An even more advanced set of channel options exist in other aspects of the car dealers' traditional business—used cars, finance and insurance, parts and service, rental and fleets.

Typically, the purchasing process involves three stages:

• Information acquisition
• Interaction experience
• Consummation of the transaction

### Information Acquisition

W.W. Grainger customers can get information from the company's on-line catalog (always open with over 189,000 products waiting to be found by the search engine), the CD-ROM catalog (over 200,000 products and 500,000 cross-references), or the traditional print catalog. They can also telephone, fax, or e-mail. Overkill? Not a bit of it; there cannot be many potential W.W. Grainger customers who have failed to find the information they require to decide whether to make, or not make, a purchase from the company.

A range of information-gathering tools makes sense. Some people need a lot of information from a great number of sources. They might prefer the information in different formats—some might prefer videos rather than brochures, for example. There are also a growing number of ways of collecting information. The fragmentation of ways of collecting and providing information alone has caused substantial segmentation of the purchasing process. For example:

- How much information do customers feel they need to have before they can make a decision?
- Do they want assistance with gathering information, or would they rather do it themselves (perhaps using a CD-ROM or the Internet)?
- Do they want a very wide choice of brands and price points or just a few?
- How important is it to the customers to feel sure that they have found the lowest possible price?

If you don't know the answers, you can be sure that some of your customers will be escaping, going elsewhere disappointed.

**Interaction Experience**

Whether it be testing the product, touching it, or examining it, customers usually require some sort of interaction before purchase. Providing a mechanism by which such interactions can be stimulated is often a useful strategy. In the car market, most car makers have relationships with rental fleets. These are not necessarily lucrative for the car makers but they ensure that people are exposed to their vehicles. (Some are starting to take this a step further with initiatives such as two-week rentals and trials, competing with aggressive rental companies—such as Sixt in

Europe, which is moving its business model back in the direction of competing with car companies.)

For some products the customer does not require physical contact as the form of interaction. Electronic shopping like Peapod is used to reduce search costs for consumers by providing product and price information on-line, allowing ordering on-line (and eventually to reduce distribution costs when critical scale is attained). The current Peapod business model unbundles the information exchange from the local grocery store but retains the physical distribution and other value-added services; the future may also unbundle the logistics from the local grocery store.

### Consummation of the Transaction

The actual purchasing transaction is no longer as simple as it once was. Over recent years, the process has become disaggregated. If you are buying a car, the transaction now encompasses such elements as finance, insurance, and several other value-added service options.

It is important to remember that the same product can be accompanied by differing approaches to information, interaction, and consummation. For example, photo finishing—a fairly standardized product—is available through various channels offering different purchasing experiences. These include mail order with limited interaction, one-hour express service with personal interaction and do-it-yourself scanning, and enlargements and the like at specialty shops.

# Segmentation by Ownership and Usage

The second form of segmentation growing in importance is that based on the ownership and usage experience. Do you want the product serviced at your home, or are you willing (in return for a discount) to take it to a service center? Do you want a loaner in the meantime? How long are you prepared to wait for service? How much product service guarantee do you want?

Obviously this dimension is different for consumables than for durable products. In the case of consumables, for example, fast food companies think about the consumption experience. You may buy fast food and eat it in your car or take it back to the office. You may want it delivered to your home or workplace. There are a myriad of kinds of consumption experience. Realizing that where people eat determines their behavior, fast food companies have designed different packaging for each experience.

More generally, there are three elements of ownership or consumption:

• *Delivery and set up.* Armstrong World Industries built a market decision support system to optimize its floor tile product offering. Consumers were segmented according to how they wanted to purchase and install the product. The first criterion was not the color of the product, as it had traditionally been, but whether customers wanted to buy and install it themselves or have it designed and installed for them. In effect, Armstrong strove to be the P&G or Wal-Mart equivalent in servicing the large building products retailer channel.

• *Service and supplies.* There are now Xerox machines you can buy, lease, or pay per click (an arrangement that includes paper and other consumables as well as the maintenance). Looking to the future, alliances between utilities and appliance manufacturers have begun to explore this idea of selling refrigeration rather than refrigerators, including equipment rental, service, financing, and even electricity in one monthly payment.

• *Replacement.* In the past, the end of the ownership experience was not systematically addressed. Brand-pull, large established customer bases, and product power meant that suppliers often made little effort to ensure that the replacement purchased was one of their products. If you bought GM the company surmised you were hardly likely to look elsewhere. Now the replacement cycle is examined with exhaustive rigor.

For example, in a range of durable products the use of leasing means that companies can contact customers three to six months before the lease is up. They can start a dialogue to understand how the customer's needs have changed.

## Channel Champions: N Brown

A company that has made a science of its channel management is N Brown, the Manchester-based U.K. mail order group. The company has an impressive record of 20 percent compound growth over the last twenty-five years. Yet the name is not immediately recognizable to many of its customers. This is because it prefers to market the brand names of its catalogs— JD Williams, Oxendales, Heather Valley, Fifty Plus, and Ambrose Wilson. In this way, customers feel they are dealing with a small and personal firm.

Each mail order catalog is targeted at a specific group of consumers. The company's success comes from the strength of its brands, backed by a marketing operation focused on a high degree of knowledge about its customers gathered through direct day-to-day contact with them. Back in the 1960s and 1970s, Sir David Alliance, the company's energetic chairman, acquired a number of small home-shopping companies and brought them all under the N Brown banner in 1972. The company has prospered by focusing on the needs of distinct customer segments of middle-aged to older consumers, especially women.

| COMPANY | N Brown | |
|---|---|---|
| ADDRESS | 53 Dale Street, Manchester, United Kingdom M60 6ES Phone: 440–161–236–8256 | |
| BUSINESS | Catalog sales | |
| STATISTICS | Employees | 1998   3,249 |
| | Annual sales (mil) | 1998   $523 |
| | Annual results (mil) | 1998   $46 |
| | Other facts | Roughly 2,300 casual clothing stores in Canada, France, Germany, Japan, the United Kingdom, and the United States |

More recently, it has also expanded into menswear, children's wear, clothes for younger women (aged thirty and under), footwear, and even home and garden products. However, the channel focus remains consistent. "We are retailing to people who prefer to shop from home," says N Brown CEO Jim Martin. Central to its success is the company's ability to manage a sophisticated database marketing process.

Via its database, the company tries to understand customers fully, to know "their tastes, their expectations of quality and their size requirements." This information, gathered from earlier purchases and from "focused selling propositions in national newspapers and magazines" is used to segment customers and tailor products and offerings accordingly, under the philosophy that "there is no such thing as the average customer."

But unlike traditional U.K. agency mail-order companies, which operate through a network of selling agents, N Brown deals directly with purchasers. In this way it has direct control over its channels. It's an approach that has served it well, and director of administration Iain MacFarlane attributes its success to the insight of chairman Sir David Alliance: "He stuck to his guns about direct shopping. He said that dealing directly with a member of a household rather than through agents will be better than an agency mail order business in the long run."[8]

The company has also developed a customer-service index, identifying more than forty critical issues in the business relationship between the company and its customers. These are used to score performance.

The company also goes to great lengths to research customer needs. For example, it recently carried out a size survey involving more than seven hundred women to improve its clothing specifications, and in turn launched a successful new catalog called "Classic Combination." In a similar vein, it has created a new footwear fitting service—Shoe Tailor.

Integral to the company's success, however, is its understanding of the special nature of the channel it operates through. Customer research shows that a key factor for customers is availability of product. N Brown keeps the highest levels of "in stock" in its industry (90 percent to 92 percent). This ensures high availability and fast delivery.

Channel Champions: N Brown (continued)

A survey among more than thirty thousand customers also revealed that they hated paying for returns. In what was an unusual step at the time, the company took the decision to offer free returns—paying the postage for customers to send clothes back.

At a cost of £2.5 million a year, the decision was not taken lightly. But the results of customer surveys indicated that the cost of returns was a major concern for customers on low incomes.

Since N Brown implemented the free returns policy, the increase in orders has outweighed the cost. Iain MacFarlane explains: "It was an act of faith really to do it. Returns went up as a result but when we analyzed what was happening sales have gone up more."

The company also recognizes that the importance of different channels is likely to change over time. This can have a major impact on the service levels required. "Transactions by telephone used to be a minuscule part of our business, it was all done on paper. With paper transactions all you could do to improve service was simplify the paperwork, there was no personalized contact. Now, 65 percent of our business is done over the phone," says MacFarlane. "It's still not the same as face-to-face, but we're speaking to customers and you can do a lot with script and training. At the end of the day, the things that matter at a distance though are goods in stock, efficient delivery and sorting out problems quickly. Those are the real issues and our customer surveys indicate we're getting better at them. In the last three years we've made strides."

In time, too, new channels including the Internet will affect the company's business. In particular, home-shopping via the Internet when it comes will mean the company could lose a degree of personal contact with its customers. It's something MacFarlane is well aware of. "We don't have any customers transacting over the Internet yet," he says. "That's still very experimental, but it will happen. It may not come until there is a very good interactive element. You're right though we could lose the personal element we have over the phone.

"The trade-off I suspect will be the efficiency of ordering and the customer confidence. Those elements will help make up for the shortfall of human interaction. Home-shopping will come.

Our advantage will be the strength of our processes and infra-structure. It's the efficiency and cost-effectiveness issue again."

*Channels from N Brown*

- Use different channels (branded mail order catalogs) to reach targeted customer segments.
- Direct contact is key to developing customer insights.
- Use new services to add value through the channel, as with free returns.
- Find out what customers really need, as with the research on sizing.

# Chapter 4

# Step Two:
# Develop New Channel Concepts

You can automate the production of cars, but you cannot automate
the production of customers.
—WALTER REUTHER[1]

Customer insights provide competitive advantage.

They offer levers of value that can be operated by the company that
develops them. For those companies that develop customer insights
there are many different ways in which value can be added—either by
sharing this knowledge with existing channel players to improve the
value pipeline or by creating new channels.

If companies know what their customers want and how and where
and why they want it, they can develop channels to meet those customer needs.

In one instance, for example, we examined gas station convenience
stores. Our client's outlets significantly underperformed other express
grocery outlets, because they failed to meet service offering needs. Generally, the relevant shopping occasions are distinct from gas purchases
and can be segmented into four types: baseload groceries, top-up groceries, snacks, and news.

Each shopping occasion required a particular mix of product and
service offerings. Baseload shoppers were looking for low prices, broad

selection, and easy parking. They wanted full grocery shopping with family-size portions. Top-up shoppers mainly wanted items like milk and bread; freshness and the cleanliness of the store were key issues for them. Snack buyers wanted a range of snacks at competitive prices, while news shoppers wanted a wide choice of magazines and easy pedestrian access.

Clearly, other outlets are better suited for some of these shopping occasions. Hypermarkets and supermarkets meet the needs for baseload grocery shopping but fail to serve snack and news shoppers well. Convenience stores meet the needs of snack shoppers very well but fail to provide the products and services for baseload grocery shopping.

Competitive analysis revealed that high margins could be realized by serving the top-up grocery segment through an express shop concept. (We also uncovered the advantages of express shops over convenience stores.)

The implications of this new approach for our client led it to make these moves:

- Concentrate on perishable items—one of the major drivers of the top-up segment.
- Continue to offer basic coverage for snack and news segments.
- Switch to family-serving package sizes, instead of the poorly performing individual-serving sizes currently in the outlets.
- Price competitively with hypermarkets and supermarkets, and below convenience stores and independent grocers.

By combining the express shop concept with a hypermarket-priced convenience store, the company could deliver an 18 percent gross margin—resulting in significant bottom-line improvement if executed successfully.

Such customer insights enable suppliers to identify the value levers in managing the supplier–channel power balance. In some cases this will involve unbundling value-added services from an existing channel or establishing alternate channels.

For example, instead of selling cars the car manufacturer could go into the business of leasing them over and over again until they are ready to be scrapped. The lease payments could be structured to include insurance, maintenance, and even running costs. The manufacturer would have the inside track on leasing the customer his or her next car and could potentially influence that process (perhaps persuading the buyer to replace the car sooner or upgrade to a higher-specification model).

Moreover, since the manufacturer would have near-perfect information on the service and accident history of the leased car, it would be able to estimate residual value accurately and would, therefore, realize more of the value of the car over its lifetime than is possible in the existing used-car retailing system, where sellers have to discount prices to reflect what buyers feel is their risk of purchasing a lemon. This is not entirely hypothetical—the increased emphasis on used vehicle programs, in both cars and trucks, is a manifestation of this phenomenon.

These sorts of issues and potential conflicts will become increasingly common in the future. Managing relationships with channels will be vital. For example, a major problem facing the computer giant Compaq is how to move from its current business model, with its network of independent dealers, to a direct sales model that more closely resembles Dell—without alienating its dealers. The smooth transfer from indirect to direct customer contact will require exceptional channel management skills. The alternative is to break with the past and accept a massive hit to revenue during the transition. These and other channel issues are repeated again and again throughout the business world.

Customer insights aim to engender loyalty. Loyal repeat customers ensure longer-lasting competitive advantage.

For new Internet-based retailers, such as Amazon.com and Peapod, an opportunity to create a successful, sustainable business model depends on the ability to build loyalty in the face of increasing competition from others—both Internet start-ups and traditional brick-and-mortar retailers selling over the Internet.

# The Monolith Unbundles

Meaningful—interactive—relationships with customers can only be built if the entire process of customer interaction is customized.

This appears obvious. But what often passes for customer care is formulaic. Recent history has seen the industrialization of service as the experience of customers has been standardized. The result is that people read from scripts and are bemused when you ask a question or depart from their carefully contrived and controlled scenario. Real customers don't role-play.

Raoul Pinnell, marketing director of the banking group NatWest, says, "Traditionally, the idea was that the bank manager had a relationship with a customer. We now have a segmented approach based on the realization that one size does not fit all. We have personal account managers, we have 24-hour a day banking, we have Action Line with automated voice response. Our proposition is that if you want to visit our branches, call us on the telephone or however you want to use our services, you can do it. This means that we have to understand that the customer is not one-dimensional. Just because a customer behaves in a certain way in one area does not mean that they will behave the same way in another situation."[2] Similarly, fast food retailers have discovered that what customers buy varies substantially if they are alone, with family, with children only, or with work colleagues.

Channel management is not about managing customers or predicting customer behavior so you can offer a standardized experience. Channel management is concerned with creating more value for customers by providing carefully differentiated and developed channels.

The most rewarding channel designs attack the issue at the level of specific customer segments or even individuals. The creation of value reflects how service needs vary among customers based on accurate and sufficiently precise understanding of customers' needs and the economics of serving those needs. Overserving the customer can be just as damaging as underserving. Providing customers with more value than they want or are willing to pay for can make a great channel concept unviable.

Effective channel management means that understanding of the customer (customer insight) and of the channel must be used by the supplier to provide the right mix—and levels of functions—to distinct customer segments in the most economic manner. Suppliers must manage channels flexibly and creatively as unbundled functions. This means using differing formats within the same channels and alternative channels to deliver the desired service and product bundles to the target customer segments. The first class passenger on an airline does not expect to stand in line to pick up tickets at the airport. The economy passenger is prepared to do so in order to keep the cost down. They share the same aircraft on the same flight, but purchase different service bundles—for which they pay different prices.

In future, we can expect to see large companies create more and more tailored product and service offerings. They will have to do so to meet different customer demands. The cost-sensitive customer won't pay for unwanted services, any more than the service-conscious customer will want the inconvenience of self-service cost savings. The upshot is a move to a menu-based approach to customer services, where you don't pay for what you don't want. This new trend is already apparent among some of the world's largest and most successful companies.

Targeted offerings fly in the face of the habitual response from companies with limited customer insight. They tend to seek to persuade customers that their products are attractive by wrapping new services around them. Instead of customizing, they relentlessly bundle everything together. More is good. One of the best examples of this is traveling by plane. If you close your eyes while flying you will find that you are at 35,000 feet, sitting in a fairly uncomfortable seat with limited leg room. The fundamental experience has not changed a great deal over the last twenty years. What has changed is the array of services wrapped around this basic product.

For an hour-long flight it is possible to take advantage of the following additional services:

• Different check-in options (no baggage check-in, electronic check-in)
• Different waiting options (executive lounge)
• A choice of newspapers
• A hot towel
• Drinks in abundance
• The in-flight entertainment
• A bed
• A motorcycle to pick you up on arrival
• A massage on the plane (provided by one airline at least)

Everything is thrown at everyone in the hope that the people who need a hot towel will be gratified and those who do not will be pleased by the in-flight entertainment. All this is done in the name of service and differentiation. There are exceptions, of course. As we have seen, some airlines are now unbundling madly to keep pace with no-frills competitors like Southwest. It is dawning on them that for some customers, less is more.

Elsewhere, however, the bundling blitz continues. The trouble with bundling more and more services around a particular channel is that its one-size-fits-all approach results in suboptimal economics. Undifferentiated bundling of services fails to recognize and leverage customer differences. It denies the individuality of consumers and delivers less and less value.

Clearly, there is an element of desperation in such bundling. Companies are fearful of what will happen if they call a halt to relentlessly following the activities of their competitors. Taken to its extreme, the result is that airlines compete on the quality of in-flight food rather than on performance measures such as punctuality—the one set of targets customers really value. Companies focus on their competitors more than on their customers. They have lost sight of their real target: customer value.

## From Customer Segments to Customer Fragments

Channel management requires companies to address narrowly defined market segments to create customized channels. The switch is from broad customer groups to customer fragments. It requires companies to rethink the way they create value. To do so, services and channel functions must be viewed as individual elements that can be combined to offer the right mix to target customers. In the auto industry manufacturers must understand local marketing, new car sales, financing, used-car trade-ins and sales, parts supply, and service. But beyond this disaggregation of major activities, they must evaluate the detailed components of these activities. Only at this level can the right services be developed for each customer fragment. For instance, the new-car selling process can be broken down into six steps:

1. Continuous, subconscious information intake from advertising, car rental experiences, observation, and so on
2. Active, focused information collection from publications, the Internet, manufacturer literature, and dealer sales personnel
3. Test drive at the dealership
4. Vehicle selection at the dealership
5. Purchase negotiations with the dealer's sales personnel
6. Post-purchase ownership, including all interactions with the dealer or manufacturer for service, repair, general customer service, and possible ongoing loan or lease payments

Each of these must be analyzed to determine how best to satisfy a particular type of car buyer and then determine who should perform each of the detailed functions needed to optimize the process from the customer's standpoint, in terms of how it feels and how much it costs. Certainly linkages across functions for different customers and for the alternative channel formats are also important.

The inevitable consequence is that more and more fragments are identified and their needs met by companies. It may in many instances provide perplexing challenges, but fragmentation is a function of recognizing that people have different expectations. The contemporary proliferation of high-quality goods and services allows suppliers to capitalize on smaller differences in customers' needs and wants.

In this environment, a larger portion of differentiation is service-related. This means that suppliers must ensure that their channels bundle the right types and variety of service elements with their products to satisfy the full range of potential target customers. Channel players that recognize and capitalize on the evolving service needs of customers and develop advantaged economics quickly gain ground. They can transform a fragment into a mass market.

Market fragmentation and the increasing complexity of many markets demand that segmentation take on a radically different role in helping to create service-based differentiation. As service and other *soft* elements delivered through the channel become more important to differentiation, manufacturers need to think more broadly about segmentation.

Segmentation, in its traditional sense, tended to concentrate on segmenting consumers by economic spending power. When GM proclaimed that it could provide a car for every pocket, it was segmenting its customers primarily by the size of their wallets.

There are many techniques for segmentation. These include product attributes, needs analysis, psychographic factors, lifestyle appeals, and so on. Fundamentally they all deal with how the customer thinks about a product while making the purchase decision.

Channel management provides a new way of looking at segmentation. It adds a fresh dimension. No longer limited to product attributes, segmentation must now include service elements such as the purchasing process and the ownership experience.

As a result, the objective of segmentation is to enable a manufacturer to design different bundles of product attributes and associated services that will better match the purchase and ownership needs and desires of different sets of consumers. To be profitable, these bundles must be tailored so that they optimize the value delivered to each customer segment while also ensuring that the bundle can be delivered economically. Making channels work requires that companies segment markets according to purchasing and ownership as well as by product. Segmentation is, therefore, a matter of increasing the opportunities customers have to interact with your product or service. Segmentation widens opportunities. It does so by determining which functions and activities are needed by which customers and then by determining how best to provide them.

## Channel Champions: Dynamically Personal Finance at Providian

The financial services industry has moved away from standardization to customization. Banking has become *personal* banking.

This leads to the confusing message that banks are capable of standardizing customization. "There is a strength that comes not only from size. It is a strength that comes from the highest standards of personal service and worldwide experience in financial markets," pronounces a Deutsche Bank advertisement, continuing, "Deutsche Bank's traditional, tailor-made approach to private banking . . . is now available . . . in 28 countries around the world. That's why private banking has a new standard worldwide."

Some are highly successful in creating a system that enables and supports customization. Providian Bancorp of San Francisco, formerly the First Deposit Corporation, is one of the largest, fastest-growing, and most profitable consumer credit companies in the United States. For four years in a row, *American Banker* has rated the company first or second on its Top 100 Earner's List for

| COMPANY | **Providian Financial Corporation** | |
|---|---|---|
| **ADDRESS** | 201 Mission Street, 28th Floor, San Francisco CA 94105 USA Phone: 415–543–0404   Fax: 415–278–6028 URL: http://www.providianfinancial.com | |
| **BUSINESS** | Financial services | |
| **STATISTICS** | Employees | 1997   4,357 |
| | Annual sales (mil) | 1997   $1,217 |
| | Annual results (mil) | 1997   $192 |
| | Other facts | Providian has five million individual accounts plus— $10 billion in credit-card balances |

## Channel Champions: Dynamically Personal Finance at Providian (continued)

banks with assets under $5 billion. Providian has built its asset base in only ten years, a success CEO Shailesh J. Mehta—an analyst by training and disposition—attributes in large part to a unique approach to marketing.

A traditional brand manager would be lost in Providian's marketing department. The first and most obvious differences are in the organization's structure. There are no brand or product managers to be seen. Instead, marketing is organized into three groups: Marketing Management, Customer Relationships, and Risk Management.

Marketing Management is, functionally, the closest parallel to a traditional brand management organization. Its charter is to identify new customers (end users) and develop new products, although the way in which it does this bears little or no resemblance to traditional marketing.

Customer Relationships is responsible for maximizing the potential from the existing customer base. This unit is further split into customer segment managers. Segments are based on customer behavior, not the more common demographic descriptors. "Demographics are not good predictors of buying behavior," Mehta maintains. "It's possible to have two demographically identical people—same sex, age, income and zip code—with totally different needs and behaviors."[3]

Risk Management handles the typical responsibilities of credit approval and portfolio risk management. Its functions are very similar to those in other financial institutions.

However, as important as these differences are, they do not reveal what may be the greatest distinction of all—a profoundly different philosophy about brands, the nature of customer relationships, and how to establish those relationships. Providian marketers do not spend their time developing brand plans or meeting with the advertising agency; instead they conduct sophisticated analyses of customer behavior. In fact, unlike many brand managers who pride themselves on their intuitive feel for the market, Providian prides itself on its state-of-the-art analytical tools that allow its marketers to track the usage patterns and profitability of each customer, setting pricing and service levels accordingly. Providian says, "We don't have marketing types, we have statisticians; 95 percent of our marketing department has an analytical background." For Providian, data and information are a vital part of the process to create knowledge-based marketing decisions.

To attract new customers, Providian begins by analyzing its own customers carefully, the logic being that they must have had a reason for choosing Providian in the first place. The focus is on identifying the behavioral characteristics that distinguish Providian customers from the market at large. Then it carefully combs the market to find customers who fit these profiles. In the last two years, Providian has expanded its original approach and also offers fee-based products to meet specific customer needs.

New product development (NPD) is one of the key roles assigned to Providian's marketing department. The company offers some of the most innovative products in the industry. However, its NPD process is very different from the classic consumer goods market-driven process.

The activities performed by Providian's Customer Relationships group have no equivalent in most marketing organizations. The group's major objective is to manage the relationship in such a way as to maximize Providian's share of the individual customer's financial services usage. It accomplishes that task by cross-selling additional products and offering differentiated service and bundled pricing.

Providian doesn't want every potential customer. Instead, it carefully selects its customers individually using proprietary and very sophisticated screening models. Customers are tracked for years before they are solicited. The selected customers are expected to be loyal to Providian. If card usage falls below target levels, Providian will deliberately raise the price, cut service levels, or in some cases actively discourage the customer by offering incentives to reduce the use of Providian's products. Providian is also focused, concentrating only on market segments it understands and is structured to serve.

In essence, Providian is offering a customer-designed product for each of its customers. Mehta is quick to note that Providian is not antibrand but views brands as a means to an end. The objective is to develop the relationships, not the brand.

Channel Champions: Dynamically Personal Finance at Providian (continued)

There is one final difference between Providian and common brand management organizations. It has no conventional market research department. Since it knows all of its customers by name and eschews most of the classic market research activities (no focus groups, no attitude surveys), there is simply no need. Furthermore, Providian's marketers are analytically competent and supported by excellent systems, which they use themselves for customer analysis. They do not need an interpreter between them and the customer base. Data fuels analysis, which creates genuine opportunities and equally genuine—and profitable—relationships with customers.

## Retail Loyalty Wars

In the retail world there are numerous examples of innovative channel concepts. The power has moved. In the United Kingdom, for example, power has shifted from manufacturers of branded goods such as Unilever to retailers such as Tesco.

Tesco has redefined itself. Tesco controls 15 percent of the $140 billion-a-year U.K. grocery industry, with sales of around $25 billion in 760 stores throughout the United Kingdom and in mainland Europe. It has transformed itself from a dull underachiever to a market leader through a series of innovations.

First, it spotted the move to larger supermarkets and developed them. Then it entered into a price war (with its Operation Check-Out). It then set the pace in customer loyalty—it was the first U.K. supermarket chain to introduce a loyalty card. It then added financial services to its loyalty package and introduced an electronic shopping operation.

Along the way it has developed its private label brands to fight off competition from discount retailers such as Aldi and Netto. Tesco was also the first supermarket chain to link its suppliers into a completely automated replenishment system and is developing an advanced scanning program with Siemens Nixdorf that will cut cashier training costs by up to 60 percent. "It is the first mover advantage," says Tesco IT director Ian O'Reily. "We know we are saving the competition a lot of trouble but we want that advantage."

It is continuing to introduce new retail formats, such as Tesco Extra—a hypermarket-style store selling a wider range of nonfood items alongside the traditional groceries. Then there is its convenience store format and the innovation, in its domestic market at least, of selling gasoline in the parking lot. "Pace, risk, progress. Those are all things that epitomise Tesco," says O'Reily.[4]

## Channel Champions: Wilsonart International

Formica Corporation popularized its decorative laminates so effectively that the company's name became synonymous with the product. It dominated the industry from its inception in 1913 until the 1970s. However, today Formica is a distant second in the $1.5 billion U.S. market.

The major reason for Formica's decline is Wilsonart (a division of Premark International). Founded in 1956, Wilsonart is presently the U.S. market leader. Although Formica enjoyed strong brand equity and economies of scale, as the industry matured and new competition entered, prices and margins came under pressure. Additionally, with expanding uses of laminates and increasing product variety, the customer base grew quite fragmented. Currently, decorative laminates are sold to many different types of customers ranging from high-volume OEMs to large commercial contractors to small handymen. These different customers naturally require quite distinct service and support. Wilsonart was able to capitalize on these market dynamics by leveraging customer service through its channel to better meet the service needs of the various market segments.

Wilsonart decided to target the residential and commercial end customer segments of the market—segments that have relatively high sensitivity to delivery time. Founded on the basis of exceptional customer service and prompt delivery, the company set out with a promise to deliver laminate anywhere in the U.S. within ten days or less. It realized that to achieve this goal an extremely effective and supportive distribution channel was needed—a tall order for a David (as it saw itself) up against a Goliath like Formica. To execute its strategy successfully, Wilsonart needed to build partnerships with distributors who would be unambiguously dedicated to customer service and satisfaction.

To serve residential and commercial customers, Wilsonart designed its entire supply chain around responsiveness. It set up a system of regional warehouses that could deliver stocked product to local distributors within a day. Its production processes were designed to turn around an order for not only non–stock items but also non–current items within ten days. If an order cannot be met within this time the customer is notified. Wilsonart continuously strives to improve the responsiveness of its extended enterprise by carefully monitoring measures such as the time that elapses between an order's clearing the last table of the manufacturing process at the plant and the time it gets to the customer.

The distribution channel is a vital part of Wilsonart's formula. Wilsonart both selects and manages its distributors in an extremely diligent manner. The company very carefully chooses distributors based on their predisposition to provide exceptional customer service, since Wilsonart believes that it is nearly impossible to change a distributor's stripes if they are not naturally committed to customer service. All its distributors are exclusive, and many owe their existence to the business assistance and financing support that Wilsonart has provided. Wilsonart has built its relationship with its channel on a simple philosophy: if at any point either the manufacturer or a distributor is dissatisfied enough, they can unilaterally end the relationship. However, it turns out that such divorces almost never occur.

Wilsonart has developed exceptionally advanced distributor management processes. The company relentlessly focuses on quantifiable drivers of distributor performance—which in turn help drive end customer satisfaction. Wilsonart explicitly defines its expectations of the distributors. Company personnel are trained to address these performance areas whenever contacting distributors. Some examples of these performance measures and typical minimum objectives for each distributor: 45 percent market share, 26 percent gross margin, eight to ten inventory turns per week, three deliveries per week to each customer, and greater than 98 percent order completion.

Distributors contribute to strategic planning activities at Wilsonart, and the company aligns its marketing strategies in different territories based on distributors' input. Distributors are also involved in a thorough annual planning exercise to develop mutually agreed performance commitments and to coordinate channel activities such as promotions. During this process, distributors are carefully evaluated in a three-day review. Wilsonart may even commission outside research to independently and objectively evaluate hard-to-determine measures such as distributors' market shares in each of several well-defined customer segments.

## Channel Champions: Wilsonart International (continued)

Product innovation had not originally been a differentiating capability for Wilsonart. In fact, the company considered itself to be a follower, albeit a fast one, in product innovation. However, with its strong ability to listen to its loyal customers, Wilsonart was encouraged by them to expand its product line to address growing end-customer needs. In response to its customers' urging Wilsonart decided to offer a product variety broader than that of any competitors, and even decided to be first in the market with solid-color laminate. This complemented Wilsonart's customer service and delivery advantages and was particularly valuable to a major portion of their target market—the commercial and high-end residential segments.

Today, Formica still remains the largest worldwide producer; however, it has been overshadowed in the U.S. market by Wilsonart (see Exhibit 4.1). It should be noted that part of Formica's fall is surely due to the numerous management and ownership disruptions that have plagued the company. Interestingly, following its latest ownership change Formica has indicated that it is concentrating on building value-added relationships with its distributors.

**Exhibit 4.1   Decorative Laminates: U.S. Market Share History**

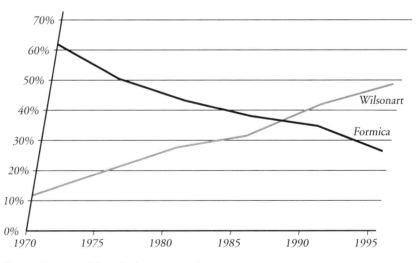

*Source:* Estimated from industry interviews.

*Channels by Wilsonart*

- *Segmentation.* Wilsonart exemplifies a channel concept focused on segments that care about customer service.
- *Responsiveness.* Wilsonart continues to succeed in growing market share in the United States because, compared to its competitors, it is much more responsive in delivering product to its end customers. Wilsonart's supply chain and channel capabilities enable it to meet customer demand within ten days (under one day for most cases).
- *Working in partnership.* Wilsonart has built a strong reputation for taking care of its distributors, which has earned it high loyalty from channel members. The distributors, in turn, are known for literally spoiling their customers with superb customer service. Wilsonart works with its channel partners to satisfy targeted customers' service needs. The constant focus on efficiency and effectiveness in the channel helps its distributors work hard to keep the end customers happy.

## Channel Champions: AutoNation Leads the Way

According to some, AutoNation may be at the forefront of the evolution of automotive retailing. AutoNation—the largest holder of new-car dealerships in the United States, parent of the AutoNation USA used-car megastore chain, and owner of multiple rental car companies—is unquestionably out in front of the pack. But we do not believe that it has, to date, demonstrated the radical changes required to excel in automotive retailing.

AutoNation is clearly a leader in first-stage channel restructuring, forcing cost reduction through aggressive rationalization and consolidation. Automotive industry observers for the most part view AutoNation as a leviathan, swallowing up auto dealers at will. For the first three quarters of 1998, AutoNation reported revenue of $12.7 billion, up 72 percent from $7.4 billion during the first three quarters of 1997. Its income from continuing operations for the same period totaled $384.2 million, up 68 percent from 1997. Automotive operations account for about 92 percent of revenue and 78 percent of operating income; solid waste services contribute the rest.

In addition, as is typical for retail innovators, AutoNation is now striving to improve the car buying and ownership experience for consumers. AutoNation announced in September 1998 that it was not going to sell cars the old-fashioned way in Denver. Under the Denver plan, AutoNation will switch to a one-price, no-haggle sales approach similar to the one pioneered by GM's Saturn division. But AutoNation goes further than Saturn. AutoNation's customers, the company announced, are to be offered membership-style benefits that will give them access to a wide range of automotive retailing, service and financing options, along with vehicle rental discounts and other related products and services. As the program develops, AutoNation says it will introduce an integrated e-commerce shopping alternative and a comprehensive customer service center. AutoNation plans to roll the program out nationwide to the more than 350 franchises it has acquired since 1995.

"Customers are tired of the high pressure, low satisfaction sales model," the company's president, Steven R. Berrard, said. "They want a simple, less time-consuming sales process. They want paperwork that's easy to understand. They want service that's done right the first time. They want a dealer who will stand behind the product, no matter where they travel. And the majority

| COMPANY | AutoNation, Inc. | |
|---|---|---|
| Subsidiaries include | Alamo Rent A Car<br>National Car Rental System<br>CarTemps USA | |
| ADDRESS | 110 SE Sixth Street, Fort Lauderdale FL 33301 USA<br>Phone: 954–769–6000   Fax: 954–769–6408<br><br>URL: http://www.autonation.com | |
| BUSINESS | Specialty retail—automobile | |
| STATISTICS | Employees | 1997   56,000 |
| | Annual sales (mil) | 1998   $17,487 |
| | Annual results (mil) | 1998   $499 |
| | Other facts | Largest car dealer in United States. Top U.S. car rental company. |

of consumers want a no-haggle, one-price selling environment—as long as they can be sure that the one price is also a competitive price."[5]

Most vehicle manufacturers in the United States and Europe have done benchmarking studies of AutoNation. Some, such as General Motors Corporation, Ford Motor Company, Mercedes Benz, and Nissan, have entered into formal franchise agreements or even business relationships with AutoNation. (In June 1998, for example, Ford agreed to partner with AutoNation to create a Ford Retail Network in Rochester, N.Y. AutoNation is running all nine dealerships in Rochester and owns 49 percent of the venture.) A few manufacturers, such as the Honda Motor Company, Toyota Motor Corporation, and Nissan Motor Company, resisted AutoNation's overtures at first in the courts and with state agencies. Yet each has come to terms in one way or another with AutoNation.

## Channel Champions: AutoNation Leads the Way (continued)

Much of AutoNation's progress so far resembles the natural evolution of retailing that has occurred in a host of other consumer-durables categories. In these categories, smart and aggressive retailers have created category-killer formats that offer both lower costs and better selection. Examples of the category killers include Home Depot (home improvement products) and Circuit City Stores (appliances and consumer electronics). (In fact, it was Circuit City that invented the CarMax Group, the first used-car superstore chain.)

Our evaluation of the growth of these category-killer formats reveals that they are characterized by significant experimentation, not necessarily by great success and profits in their early development. However, once the format is perfected, these retailers rapidly replicate outlets in many markets. When observers look at the financial teething pains of AutoNation and argue that they are stumbling and will stop expanding, they ignore the lessons of the past.

AutoNation's used-car business provides an illustration of this early-phase adaptation process. Over the past two years the increasing supply of used sedans and heightened used-car retail competition have driven prices down, requiring AutoNation to significantly improve its retail operations. AutoNation has reduced its store staffing by an average of about 20 percent, fine-tuned its reconditioning economics and vehicle assortment, and has brought in new management to further perfect and roll out the format. Despite the price pressure, sales have been increasing at an ever-increasing rate, as illustrated in Exhibit 4.2.

The second stage of retail evolution is driven by the recognition, again usually by smart retailers rather than manufacturers, that consumers differ in the way they want to buy and own their products. This leads to the creation of multiple formats and distribution channels, each with tailored bundles of services and associated economics. These formats can coexist with each other over time, because consumers select the format best suited to their needs. These can range from exclusive brand and very high service to minimal service, broad selection, and low prices.

For example, Home Depot is attempting to capture additional market segments with new channels and formats, such as its

**Exhibit 4.2   AutoNation Sales**

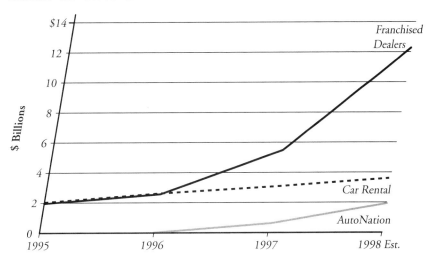

Expo design format, local hardware stores, home installation services, and Internet sales. In the consumer-durables categories, the
category-killer format typically captures 30 percent to 40 percent
of the market, leaving most of the rest spread among two or three
other formats.

AutoNation appears to recognize these second-stage requirements, at least in used cars. In April 1998, AutoNation acquired
Driver's Mart Worldwide. The Driver's Mart concept is different
from AutoNation's, with more participation by the local operator,
improved selling and reconditioning processes, and smaller lots
with lower inventory. AutoNation has also experimented, through
AutoNation, with a format called Value Stop (older cars, lower
prices) and a dedicated AutoNation branded center in Houston
for used trucks, vans, and sport utility vehicles.

The third stage of retail evolution involves changing the
fundamental retailing paradigm. The prevailing paradigm in the
automotive industry is that car companies design and build cars
while dealers distribute and service them. An alternative paradigm
is that car manufacturers are in the business of creating economic
assets that must be managed over the life of the assets to create

Channel Champions: AutoNation Leads the Way (continued)

and capture value. Leasing forces manufacturers to confront this new paradigm, because the cars stay on the books of their captive finance companies, and some of the more creative automakers are beginning to think about how to exploit its value more fully. With its extensive business base and multiple automotive operations (dealerships, used-car megastores and rental cars), AutoNation has capacity to test and lead such new concepts as few others in the industry can. AutoNation also brings other critical elements to the party—an outsider's perspective and an innovative spirit.

To date AutoNation has focused primarily on pursuing the benefits of consolidation typical in the first stage of retail channel evolution. Exhibit 4.3 sketches its current business system setup. But some of its actions suggest the potential for truly game-changing retail evolution. When channel players, as op-

**Exhibit 4.3   AutoNation, National, and Alamo Business System**

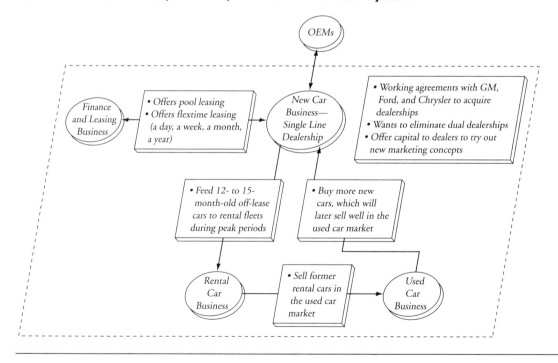

posed to manufacturers, are the winners in retail evolution, most often the one that leads in the first stage is the one that leads in other stages and reaps substantial benefits. AutoNation could be the first in the automotive industry to create an independent retail brand that actually "owns the customer."

*Channels by AutoNation*

- Redefine your business beyond the traditional transaction selling paradigm.
- Continuously experiment and refine your channel formats and operations.
- Acquire and partner in channels to expand your offerings and learnings.

# Chapter 5
# Step Three: Pilot Test

The best way to have a good idea is to have lots of ideas.
—Dr. Linus Pauling[1]

Whether a channel is completely new or a carefully evolved network, it's a good idea to pilot test before plunging in.

Pilot testing the new channel enables you to refine the economics and competitive positioning of the channel concepts—structures, services, and operational systems. Ideally, pilot tests are insulated as much as possible from the main business. This is primarily to minimize the likelihood of an anticipatory reaction by customers or suppliers. The test should be on the market periphery to minimize reactions from competitors until the business model you are seeking to develop is robust.

## Setting Up a Test

In pilot testing a channel concept, a number of issues need to be considered:

*Core team.* There needs to be a core team with overall responsibility for making the pilot work and for monitoring and garnering insights from the experience.

*Identification of hosts.* Identifying which areas of the business are to host the pilot is crucial. Clearly, some offer better chances of success and of learning than others.

It is important to establish clear criteria for selection so that a short list (four or five possibles) can be generated. Criteria may include aspects such as geography, market potential, propensity for change, energy and skill of executives and staff, and local infrastructure.

*Identification of resources.* Pilot tests require human and financial resources. The degree of these commitments clearly varies from test to test. They need to be clearly delineated. All costs must also be weighed against measures of potential benefits.

In one pilot program we worked on, twelve to fourteen people worked full time overseeing the initiative. Responsibilities were split along the following lines: there was a core team and steering committee generally consisting of eight people, plus a single overall program manager, one manager responsible for communication strategy, one for roles, responsibilities, and incentives, one for selecting the pilot businesses, and another to take care of day-to-day running issues.

In terms of human resources it is important to adhere to a number of basic principles:

- The best people should work on the pilot—not the ones who are easiest to free up.
- A dedicated staff group with a single-minded focus on making the pilot work is preferable to part-time commitment and part-time belief.
- The staff should be chosen for the ability to perform detailed, execution-oriented work, rather than for specialized knowledge or control of resources.
- The pilot program needs a built-in protective system so that selected staff are not pulled back into their prior responsibilities.
- Other essential staff characteristics include enthusiasm, entrepreneurial spirit, creative problem-solving ability, ability to adapt quickly to change, and perseverance and ability to overcome barriers.

*Communication.* Communication in simple and clearly under-standable language is essential at all stages. The entire process should be one of discussion and feedback. There should be continual discussion between the core team and those involved in the test. In particular, communication should reinforce belief in the pilot test and the underlying concept. It should also highlight significant wins and progress.

Internal communications start with awareness building in the initial stage—this positions the initiative from a strategic perspective, reaffirms company principles, provides specifics on what is going to happen, and announces top management support. During the pilot test internal communication focuses on giving details of the status of the project—the emphasis is on demonstrating top management commitment to the efforts, reaffirming the strategic rationale, outlining the framework and process in use, and highlighting progress and wins. Finally, if the pilot is rolled out, the communications emphasis is on top management commitment, the rationale and implications of broader implementation, and details of training.

The overall emphasis should be on rapid feedback. This is facilitated by limiting the number of pilot tests to two or three, giving those involved authority to change and adapt parameters as they progress, and establishing a clearly defined feedback process.

All communication should be consistent with some basic principles:

- *Link messages to strategic purpose and direction.* This puts the program in context so that employees understand the need for it and credibility is built into the process.
- *Be honest and open.* This is critical to maintaining credibility. (Open does not mean that all information needs to be available to everyone every step of the way. But it does mean that all participants need honest feedback via official channels about the state of the test, whether it's going well or badly; the rumor mill will certainly carry the latter information, and sponsors will lose all credibility if they stray too far from reality.)
- *Set realistic expectations.* Potential implications need to be mapped out early on without glossing over potentially negative messages,

and parameters and limits should be shared to prevent the anticipation of worst-case outcomes.

- *Provide for two-way communications.* There should be opportunities for employees to submit the questions they really have and to provide their ideas.
- *Emphasize being proactive rather than reactive.* Messages need to be sent out in advance, before there is a great hue and cry. Defensiveness needs to be avoided.
- *Send the same messages repeatedly through alternative channels.* Frequently individuals need to hear a message several times before they internalize it. Using multiple channels increases the chances of this happening.

*Identification of the process.* Pilot tests cannot exist in a vacuum. If participants believe the pilot will not lead to wider initiatives it is dead in the water. As a result, a clear process needs to be mapped out and communicated.

Generally, the first stage of the pilot test must give it a jump start and beginning momentum. The emphasis should be on establishing direct communication with all stakeholders and defining roles, responsibilities, and incentives. At this stage it is useful to develop a vision for the pilot that identifies the framework, process, required analyses, and key program elements. The next stages need also to be carefully detailed and their timing and content communicated.

The second stage actually sees the pilot test in operation. The emphasis here should be on tracking, monitoring, and measuring.

Finally, the value of the pilot—measured against agreed objectives—needs to be decided on.

*Awareness of pitfalls.* Making change happen is always difficult, sometimes impossible. It is important to identify potential pitfalls and obstacles to making a pilot work. It should be remembered, for example, that people are creatures of habit and risk-averse. Also, the required competencies and confidence may be lacking. Incentives may be required. At the same time, it needs to be continually reinforced that change demands significant commitment and investment and that tangible results will take time to materialize.

## Channel Champions: Wal-Mart

By 1988 Europe was sprinkled with an increasing number of what were labeled *hypermarkets.* The idea for this retailing format came from the European retailer Carrefour in 1962. By 1988 it ran 73 hypermarkets throughout Europe and, overall, there were 780. The idea behind hypermarkets was straightforward: the stores sold grocery and other general goods under one, admittedly large, roof. Customers could load up with their week's groceries and buy some clothes or household items at the same time.

At the time, there were a number of U.S. chains offering this sort of combo shopping—including Fred Meyer and Meijer. Wal-Mart, the dominant general merchandise retailer, eyed the possibilities with increasing enthusiasm. Opening a combined

| COMPANY | **Wal-Mart Stores, Inc.** | |
|---|---|---|
| Subsidiaries include | North Arkansas Wholesale Co., Inc., Bentonville, Arkansas<br>Wal-Mart Realty Company, Bentonville, Arkansas<br>McLane Company, Inc., Temple, Texas<br>Cifra S.A. de C.V. (51 percent), Mexico City, Mexico | |
| ADDRESS | 702 SW Eighth Street, P.O. Box 116, Bentonville AR 72712 USA<br>Phone: 501–273–4000   Fax: 501–273–1917<br><br>URL: http://www.wal-mart.com | |
| BUSINESS | General merchandising | |
| STATISTICS | Employees | 1998   910,000 |
| | Annual sales (mil) | 1998   $137,634 |
| | Annual results (mil) | 1998   $4,430 |
| | Other facts | Brand names: Sam's Club, Hypermart USA, Bud's Warehouse Outlets |

merchandise and grocery operation would give it access to the fragmented grocery sector and, hopefully, improve performance in the discount general merchandise sector. Combining the two offered the chance to continue the company's rapid expansion. At the time, Wal-Mart controlled 50 percent of the $150 billion discount store business. Another 32 percent of the industry was controlled by K-mart and Target. Any further inroads into market share were going to be difficult to achieve.

Grocery retailing, in contrast, was alluring. Wal-Mart saw that this $400 billion industry was extremely intriguing—and fragmented. The largest supermarket chain, Krogers, controlled a mere 6 percent of the market and the top ten combined only mustered 19 percent of the market.

The downside of grocery retailing was simply that margins were low. Expansion was possible, but focused grocery outlets would always be handicapped by the industry's poor margins. But Wal-Mart saw a more positive message in the picture— consumers visit grocery stores more regularly than general merchandise stores; if the opportunity was there for custom- ers to cross the aisle and buy some general merchandise, the conundrum of low margins in the grocery business and intense competition in general merchandising could be solved.

In 1987 Wal-Mart had tested the water with Hypermart USA. It brought in grocery experts and brought some grocery companies in as partners—this culminated in the 1991 purchase of McLane & Co., a grocery and general merchandise wholesaler.

At the same time as it was assembling the necessary expertise, Wal-Mart moved on with three more hypermarkets in the next few years. The stores were enormous—220,000 square feet—complex, costly, and low on profits. But the company was happy to accept that these were pilot tests for the real thing. The emphasis was on fast learning and slow growth with lots of adjustments and fine- tuning along the way.

The first Hypermarts provided a variety of lessons. These were taken on board when Wal-Mart opened its first Supercenter in Washington, Missouri, in March 1988. The new store was smaller than the Hypermart format. More followed. Over the next two years, five more Supercenters were built in Missouri, Oklahoma, and Arkansas. The smallest was 90,000 square feet, the biggest 170,000.

With six Supercenters and four Hypermarts up and running, the pilot process was under way so that Wal-Mart could fully understand the potential business proposition and likely problems in introducing the combo format. One notable challenge was posed by inventory. Wal-Mart was used to carrying a full sixty days of inventory in general merchandising. In the grocery business, twenty-five days of inventory was normal—less than ten days for meat and other fresh produce. In response, Wal-Mart increased its inventory management capabilities and created manufacturing systems in certain areas.

Pilot tests of this magnitude do not come cheap. It took four years of experimentation before Wal-Mart took the plunge into Supercenters. Between 1992 and 1998, it built 558 such stores. Roll-out was rapid. Every single store built on the lessons learned in the pilot phase of the early 1990s.

For example, Wal-Mart developed its own food distribution network—rather than relying on other distributors—and its engineers and construction team learned from grocery store professionals to construct stores that were suitable to this new use and cheaper than those built by the competition. Test marketing continues even now so that learning and improvement are ongoing.

The end result is that Wal-Mart had 1998 grocery sales of $32 billion, making it the third-largest supermarket operator—projected to become the largest by 2002. In 1999, Wal-Mart plans to open 150 further Supercenters, with 90 replacing existing discount stores. The mutually beneficial relationship between grocery and general merchandise has largely been confirmed. Superstores have 30 percent greater general merchandise sales than their discount store counterparts.

Wal-Mart is now piloting another new format. This is Wal-Mart Neighborhood Markets, 40,000-square-foot stand-alone supermarkets. Three have now been opened.

---

### Channels by Wal-Mart

- Plan on slow growth in the pilot test phase.
- Structure the pilot test for extensive learning and concept retirement.
- Invest enough in the pilot test to ensure that insufficient resources do not bias the results and that adequate concept investigation occurs.
- Dedicate company employees to the pilot test, to learn and capture key insights for roll-out.

---

# SPODs with Everything

In the early 1990s, despite the fact that it was continually setting new quarterly sales records, the burger giant McDonald's found its market share declining. It had dropped from 18.8 percent in 1986 to 16.2 percent in 1990 and was still sliding.[2] The company had to do something, but this would be a difficult task. Although it owned 40.4 percent of the American burger business in 1993, there was little comfort in that— the segment was generally much slower-growing than the newly popular pizza and ethnic foods segments.

McDonald's wanted to create a strategy to aggressively add outlets and different types of stores to recapture the market share it lost in the late eighties. But where would it look? It decided to expand its channels to nontraditional ones like convenience stores and gas stations. Through alliances with Wal-Mart and major oil companies, McDonald's was able to test its expanding Special Points of Delivery (SPODs) through well-organized and established means.

The fast food and gas combo was popping up all over the United States. Across the country, Taco Bell, Subway, Burger King and Kentucky Fried Chicken went into partnership with big gasoline companies like Chevron, Texaco, Amoco, Exxon, and Unocal. "Our alliance with petroleum companies means the ultimate in convenience," McDonald's announced. "At these locations, you'll find a full-menu McDonald's restaurant with fast service, along with a service station and a convenience store! Nothing could be more convenient, because you can fill up your car, buy a meal and pick up items for your home with just one stop."[3]

McDonald's joined the throng and also expanded its express outlets in or attached to other retail operations. Through a two-pronged approach, the chain targeted satellite and kiosk operations as well as traditional stores in its development plan. Edward Rensi, then president and chief executive for domestic operations, noted that the company was aiming for a 7 percent market share in nontraditional outlets, which would amount to an additional $3 billion in sales.

At McDonald's, much of the move toward nontraditional channels seemed to be driven by two factors. The first was the scarcity of prime sites for traditional free-standing units. The second was the desire of both the fast food operator and the partnering business to share operating costs and gain venues for products alongside those of other strong brands that are attractive to consumers.

The industry saw many opportunities for new nontraditional channels and points of distribution. Hospitals, sports arenas, and roadways were some prime examples. "Any branded food operators that wanted to get into the C-store business would not find a better time or a more fertile ground than there is now," said Jim Mitchell, president of Mitchell Design Group, in 1994. For travelers, the cobranded outlets at gas stations were a new type of one-stop shopping. For franchisees and gas station dealerships, it meant lower start-up costs and shared expenses.

Some in the industry predicted double-digit growth for the segment. There are many additional benefits to these SPOD restaurants. Airports, for example, are a great source of learning, says Bob Scanlon, VP for SPODs for Quizno's. "Airports teach you how to be much more efficient. Airport real estate is expensive, so concessionaires must learn how to present their concept efficiently in smaller locations. Lessons learned from airport franchises can be applied throughout the chain as well. Companies are focusing on the needs of the traveler, such as speed, convenience, access and a quality product, then apply those concepts to their traditional stores."[4] Scanlon also sees airport locations as "bill-boards" for his street-level locations. Another industry exec feels that business is increased by moving closer to the consumer. "The closer you get the product to the consumer, the more you'll sell of it," says David Hawthorne of Lewis Foods. Additionally, these expansions just mean more market penetration for the franchise owners.

McDonald's development of the SPOD channel began in January 1993, when it opened a scaled-down restaurant in a Wal-Mart store in Visalia, California. By the year end, approximately seventy restaurants were operated in Wal-Mart stores—and by the end of 1995 there were around four hundred satellite facilities. McDonald's went on to open restaurants in a variety of nontraditional locations, including airports, trains, cruise ships, zoos, museums, tollway plazas, college campuses, hypermarkets, and department stores. An early attempt at an airport SPOD had moderate success because of an extremely limited menu. In spite of the regular appearance of the facility, there were hot dogs rather than burgers. Discussions with Home Depot resulted in the availability of Big Macs in some of their home centers.[5] Other unique SPODs include serving children's Happy Meals on United Airlines flights, aboard Swiss Federal Railways trains and an English Channel ferry, and in an ice skating rink in Wisconsin.

For McDonald's the two key alliances were with Chevron and Amoco. At the end of 1997, McDonald's had developed sixty-eight co-branded locations with Chevron, most in the Western and Southwestern region of the United States, and eighty-nine shared locations with Amoco in the Midwestern, Mid-Atlantic, North Central, and Southeastern regions of the country. These sites consisted of restaurant, gas station, and convenience store.

McDonald's total satellite growth was very fast through the mid-1990s, but slowed and reduced into 1996 and 1997. At the end of 1993, McDonald's had 170 satellites operating around the world—with plans to add hundreds every year. By year-end 1994 that number reached 745 and in 1995, 1,571. In 1996 the company stated that it would begin refocusing its growth on traditional units rather than the anticipated growth of satellite facilities. In fact, in 1997, 115 low-volume U.S. satellite restaurants were closed to reduce ongoing costs and to strengthen the U.S. business.

It appears that the new channels have not been as profitable as once envisioned. The existing satellite restaurants in convenience store–gas station combinations are posting mixed results and some believe they will dilute the McDonald's brand. Those people say that the effect of a McDonald's Express in a C-store is to downgrade the real McDonald's. Others believe that the convenience store industry (which posted $132.2 billion in sales, selling gasoline in 72 percent of its locations) is ripe for overhauls that would involve adding more up-to-date elements, like fast-food brands or some other type of food court.[6]

Some anticipate further potential problems down the road. "Teaming up with several different players in the convenience store–gas station business stands to present new operational challenges for McDonald's that haven't surfaced yet in the company's joint venture with Wal-Mart. Wal-Mart works because it is operated by one company," said Dick Adams, president of Franchise Equity Group.[7] Another pitfall of these facilities is the higher cost of the location. For a shared space, McDonald's is often forced to lease space as opposed to owning the space, which is typical for traditional facilities.

Accordingly, original plans have since been scaled back, but McDonald's still has some focus on these smaller points of distribution. From a channel management perspective, the lessons may be that the company spent too little time pilot testing. On the plus side, the roll-out of the new concept was rapid and McDonald's has, in the face of mixed results, shown a willingness to adapt the concept as time goes on and experience accumulates.

# Chapter 6
# Step Four: Rapid Roll-Out

When skating over thin ice our safety is in our speed.
— RALPH WALDO EMERSON[1]

Making channels happen requires rapid roll-out of the concepts across segments and geographies.

Having completed the pilot test step, the challenge is to quickly start to realize the benefits of the new channel proposition on a broad scale. The pilot test step should either raise so many issues and concerns that the program is clearly revamped or generate the insight and confidence to proceed as rapidly as possible in roll-out.

Often the competitive advantage of a new channel concept comes from being first. Typically, at a high level, the ideas can be readily identified and copied. Therefore, getting far ahead of the competition in terms of refining the small details and simply being the first is critical for gaining the upper hand. This accumulated knowledge and head start are then surprisingly difficult to replicate.

For instance, the phenomenal success of channel champions such as Wal-Mart and Home Depot comes from the myriad of operational practices they developed and then the speed with which they expanded their businesses. Many others have analyzed these success stories, but no competitors have come close in matching them.

## Channel Champions: The Home Depot

An excellent example of rapid roll-out is The Home Depot. The American retail do-it-yourself chain's value creation is the result of a very simple model: growing very high return businesses at incredible speed.

The company has grown at an annual average rate of 50 percent over the past decade. At the same time, its ROS and ROCE have remained fairly constant at 20 percent. Its sales grew from $118 million in 1982 to $7.1 billion in 1992 and to $30.2 billion in 1998. Twenty-seven quarters of consecutive record sales and record earnings have pushed its stock price higher at a compound annual rate of over 70 percent for the last eight years. Underlying this success is aggressive roll-out of a powerful channel strategy that combines high volume, excellent customer service, and low prices stemming from a sophisticated logistics system. And not only has the profitable asset base grown rapidly, but the cash cost of the growth has been relatively inexpensive because of ever-increasing experience in opening new stores.

The Home Depot has been adding forty to fifty new stores every year. The company is now expanding into new geographic markets such as the U.S. Northeast as well as California and Florida.

| COMPANY | The Home Depot, Inc. | |
|---|---|---|
| ADDRESS | 2455 Pace Ferry Road, Atlanta GA 30339–4024 USA<br>Phone: 770–433–8211   Fax: 770–384–2337<br><br>URL: http://www.homedepot.com | |
| BUSINESS | Specialty retail—home improvement | |
| STATISTICS | Employees | 1998   157,000 |
| | Annual sales (mil) | 1998   $30,219 |
| | Annual results (mil) | 1998   $1,614 |
| | Other facts | More than 760 stores.<br>Largest home-improvement<br>retailer in United States. |

The Home Depot's timing was right. It caught the decline in new home building and the shift toward the name-branded do-it-yourself and buy-it-yourself market. In addition, it faced limited competition from local lumberyards and a few historically unsophisticated home center chains, many of which simply operated regionally.

To this The Home Depot brought a new approach, new capabilities and new benefits for customers. It did so in a variety of ways:

- Using a large warehouse format
- Providing excellent in-store service designed for end consumers (as opposed to building contractors)
- Leveraging scale for price and cost advantages
- Applying consumer-oriented merchandising capabilities and product variety previously not available in its industry
- Using superior inventory and information management (compared to most of its competition)

The Home Depot has continued to up the ante. It has piled the pressure on traditional wholesale distributors, specialty stores, lumberyards, and hardware stores, and especially on other home centers. It has done so by continually adding new services and products, offering installation services, introducing contractor services with separate contractor desks and credit services that serve the contractor segment of the market, and introducing its own private label products.

Interestingly, the growth of home centers illustrates the challenges faced by manufacturers and other distributors in a channel evolution when roll-out is fast and successful. Home centers now provide an increasing customer base with a growing product–service offering at ever-improving value—they represent the leading edge in building products retailing. Large chains, with their growing power, exert more and more influence over many suppliers, most of whom have been forced to react to the changes instead of anticipating and preparing for them.

As we have seen in other retail sectors, as chains become larger they become more sophisticated and more powerful. Their power and roll-out prowess is demonstrated in different ways. Some expand their geographic market focus. Others target services at specific segments. They might offer more specialized programs for the trade or professional markets. Alternatively, they might

## Channel Champions: The Home Depot (continued)

target female customers, move into installed sales (43 percent of chains report having an installed sales program and 48 percent of those use their own personnel), offer home delivery or rental programs.

The details embedded in their roll-out models typically include smart merchandising concepts. Once again the possibilities are numerous:

- Improved displays, packaging, and literature or videos including computerized sizing, pricing, and order entry systems for customers
- More direct product profitability measures
- Improved inventory management and responsiveness to changing customer demand, employing bar code scanning and computer-to-computer purchasing from suppliers
- Expanded design services and computer-aided product selection
- Better sales training
- Expanded and more sophisticated promotions
- More private labeling
- Specialty department formats

Home centers expect and demand improved support from suppliers. They expect better fill rates, increased cooperation, better returned merchandise programs, shorter lead times, and a host of other things. Clearly, this presents suppliers with important challenges and opportunities. Some manufacturers may be able to leverage existing capabilities to meet home center needs. They might, for example, be able to customize products for home centers or proactively manage and assist home centers through merchandising and promotions. Large multiline suppliers may be able to take advantage of scale to preempt or create barriers for other suppliers.

*Channels from The Home Depot*

- Roll out rapidly and dominate markets as you expand.
- Maintain pressure during the roll-out by evolving and adapting the product–service offering.
- Leverage your suppliers to economically extend your geographic network.

There are four major elements of successful rapid roll-out. First is the strategic planning this involves, making the high-level decisions that determine resource levels, risks, target roll-out areas, and timing—in other words, the overall game plan. This strategic planning element must balance the risks and resources against the objective of extremely rapid roll-out.

The second element is tactical planning. The tactical level involves systematic (often based on a specific formula) selection of where and when to roll out. For example, the tactical questions include which city to choose for the next implementation, how many outlets a particular city needs, or which specific locations to use. Over time learning and applying the exact combination of variables that optimize these decisions becomes very valuable.

The third element is executional methodology. Once a target city or site is selected, all of the vast number of specific tasks required to implement the channel concept constitute the executional phase. Since channel champion success often stems from getting many, many details right, the executional elements are obviously crucial.

A repeatable routine is the key. This routine must be more than a general understanding of the process that resides in a few people's heads. It needs to be a written set of clear, detailed instructions that multiple teams can use simultaneously to implement the roll-out in different places.

The fourth major roll-out element is monitoring and measurement. The strategic planning element should establish clear, quantifiable goals and milestones for roll-out. Progress and performance must be rigorously monitored against these plans and course corrections made accordingly.

These four elements all contribute to a successful roll-out. Along the way, however, it remains necessary to be alert for some common mistakes, and to correct them promptly if they arise. Roll-outs often fail due to errors like these:

- Failing to apply sufficient resources early in the process—especially, failing to engage key roll-out personnel in the pilot test phase
- Failing to anticipate and prepare for problems such as legal barriers to the implementation plan, or conflict with other channels

- Ignoring lessons learned in the pilot test phase
- Losing focus on target customers or other parts of the business in the effort to meet quantifiable roll-out objectives
- Failing to establish and use milestones for course correction decisions

Wal-Mart took its time pilot testing the Supercenter concept, but once it was sure of its potential expanded rapidly.

# Chapter 7

# Step Five: Study the Results and Adapt Your Channel

> Increasingly, the art of management is managing knowledge. That means we do not manage people per se, but rather the knowledge that they carry. And leadership means creating the conditions that enable people to produce valid knowledge and to do so in ways that encourage personal responsibility.
> —CHRIS ARGYRIS[1]

Companies and channels fail when learning comes to an end.

Learning and evolution are necessary for survival. But, inevitably, learning isn't easy. It flounders for a number of reasons:

- *Lack of top management commitment.* Real engagement of the top management team is necessary to gain the commitment required. Top managers must invest enough time to gain a real understanding of the issues, the people's concerns, and what is actually going on. They must engage their instincts as well as their intellects. This is especially true when venturing into new channels.

- *Self-restricted options.* Most managers reach the top by succeeding in the box. They do not think differently. They do not readily embrace alternative, out of the box, thinking. Concepts are best created from seeds that are outside the box. Multiple seeds create more concepts. (The process is easier if the seeds can be justified by a sound business case.)

- *Inability to learn from experience.* As Harvard's Chris Argyris points out, companies are remarkably inept at learning from experience. Indeed, experience is one of the great mysteries of organizational life. It is assumed that managers benefit from experience. More experience enables better decisions (though only if you learn from experience). But while personal experience is recognized as important, collective corporate experience tends to be overlooked.

- *Inflexibility and lack of authority.* Learning requires flexibility and a willingness to risk something new—plus the authority to try it and the security to face failure constructively. Unfortunately, most managers are ill at ease with the entire idea of learning from their mistakes. Another uncomfortable insight from Chris Argyris is that managers are more likely to attempt to sweep a mistake under the corporate carpet than take it out into the open and attempt to learn from it. This kind of reaction is rational in the usual corporate environment, where anything less than perfect success can blight a career, but it also makes innovation very difficult—pilot programs are worthless without learning. Many companies waste a great deal of effort on attempts to share responsibility and blame, rather than allowing people to try potentially useful things and profit by the experience of what doesn't work as well as what does.

◆ ◆ ◆

Any new idea requires development to overcome the host of practical objections. It is important that ideas aren't eliminated too quickly. The emphasis should be on maintaining divergent views until alternative concepts are developed. To develop a new idea, a company needs managers skilled at several difficult but essential tasks:

- *Dealing with uncertainty.* The learning organization creates uncertainty and ambiguity in areas that were previously clear. Managers must learn to manage in this more nebulous and less easily understood environment. Programs of change are similarly fraught with uncertainty.

- *Accepting responsibility.* Individuals must take responsibility for learning. They cannot blame others for a lack of development opportunities—they must pursue and create their own.

- *Learning new skills.* In particular, managers must develop listening skills and be able to act as facilitators. Simply dictating adds no learning value.
- *Developing trust.* Reared on the concept of divide and rule, many managers find that trusting people does not come easily.

# Strategic Breakouts

Despite the myriad of structural and human factors that make it difficult for companies to learn, learn they must. Learning is the route to linking the launch of new channel concepts to Step One of the channel management process, understanding customer needs. Learning is the route to what Charles Lucier, Leslie Moeller, and Raymond Held label *strategic innovation.*[2]

Strategic innovations are not brilliant insights. Instead, they are powerful value propositions rooted in an advantaged business model developed through experience. Nor are they written on tablets of stone. The ultimately successful concept is usually radically different from the one that starts the process moving. Usually the business model and value proposition require significant adaptations based on learning over time.

Strategic innovations are rare because the thinking process behind them is unfamiliar. Traditional strategic planning reduces the likelihood of a breakout. Few strategic breakouts occur in companies with strong strategic planning processes. The emphasis of strategic planning tends to be on incremental improvement. The process moves from fact finding through strategy formulation to programming; planning for breakout moves from fact finding through what is labeled ideation to learning in doing. In addition, strategic innovations are especially difficult for established players whose mind-set tends to be grounded in the here and now and who are concerned about the cannibalization of the existing business.

Lucier and his colleagues analyzed shareholder value creation at more than 1,300 large companies publicly traded in the United States from 1972 to 1996. They also explored case studies of 65 companies in the top 10 percent of shareholder value creation for at least a decade.

Exhibit 7.1 lists the leaders as revealed in this research. One critical conclusion was that companies that achieve strategic innovation earn superior returns for their shareholders.

The research found that over 80 percent of the past strategic innovations studied resulted from the application of one of four concepts:

- Power retailing: Circuit City, The Home Depot
- Bypassing steps in the industry value chain: Tyson's, Frito Lay, Dell
- Focusing and removing complexity: Southwest Airlines; Nucor
- Fully leveraging brands: Walt Disney; Coca-Cola

The research confirmed that strategic innovations don't happen very often. In seventy-five industries in the United States over forty years, only 1.3 companies per decade, per industry, attempted strategic breakout. Nearly half (0.6 per industry, per decade) succeeded, creating significant competitive advantage for at least five years for the innovator. (Successes include Wal-Mart, Home Depot, Southwest Airlines, Federal Express.) Most of the remaining attempts were partially successful. Either the innovation transformed only one segment of the industry rather than its entirety or the innovator gained only a transitory advantage—such as airline reservation systems.

Learning—and the knowledge of learning—has provided a variety of tools and methodologies that enable breakouts. These include sce-

**Exhibit 7.1    Top 10 Percent Returns to Shareholders Over at Least a Decade**

| Company | Industry | Current Sales ($billion) | Time Period |
|---|---|---|---|
| Wal-Mart | Discount retailing | 137.6 | 1970–early 1990s |
| The Home Depot | Home center retailing | 30.2 | 1980–early 1990s |
| Waste Management | Waste management | 12.7 | 1975–1994 |
| Circuit City | Appliance retailing | 8.0 | 1970–1992 |
| Tyson's Foods | Chicken processing | 7.4 | 1970–1990 |
| Nucor | Steel | 4.2 | 1970–1992 |
| Shaw Carpets | Floor coverings | 3.5 | 1975–present |
| Great Lakes Chemical | Specialty chemicals | 1.4 | 1975–present |

nario-based planning, war games, lateral thinking, and the various popular creative processes used by managers.

Key lessons from the research into strategic innovation:

- *They are not isolated occurrences.* Instead, they grow out of a lengthy process stretching over years rather than months, and it is essential to recognize that a powerful business model takes a long time to create. However, significant financial returns will begin during replication of the business model—especially returns to shareholders.
- *They need pilot testing.* The value proposition and business model will not be right until you gain real-world experience.
- *Once refined, they can be rolled out rapidly.* Incorporate learning from pilot tests as quickly as possible to adjust the value proposition and business model.

But the central lesson is that of learning in doing, the development through experience of a dramatically superior value proposition and business model. Learning in doing means that learning is driven by experience fed back through refinements of the business model. The more rapid the feedback and the more frequent and effective the refinements to the value proposition and business model, the shorter the period of learning in doing.

From a managerial perspective, breakouts present three key challenges:

First, there has to be commitment. Aspirations must be high, and participants need to accept the risks involved and be willing to wait patiently for benefits. All this takes time and attention.

Second, this commitment has to be maintained over several years. Assuring the success of strategic innovation can require pilot tests to be run over several years. This runs the risk of cannibalizing the existing businesses. Faced with the usual array of short-term problems and challenges, managers can easily regard pilot tests as being of secondary importance unless the corporate environment includes proper safeguards for long-range innovation.

Third, breakouts demand differentiation management. They need distinct and different measurements. And these measurements need to be communicated and refined; there has to be a constantly maintained and open direct link from top management to the pilot tests and back.

## Channel Champions: Windows by Pella

Pella Corporation is one of the leading U.S. manufacturers of fenestration products (windows, doors, and skylights). Founded in 1925, the company built a reputation for top-quality, meticulously crafted wood products targeted at the high end of the market. Pella also flourished based on its market innovations including a roll-up window screen (its initial product); between-glass options such as blinds; and aluminum-clad, maintenance-free windows.

Until the latter part of the 1980s, Pella was growing at an average annual rate of over 9 percent.[3] It was one of the largest window makers in a highly fragmented industry. Pella had a distinct premium position with a strong brand name, and it enjoyed double-digit market share in the wood window, custom home segment. However, even though the market had been growing for several years, Pella's revenues had begun to flatten. Additionally, the market was changing fundamentally. Conse-

| COMPANY | Pella Corporation | |
|---|---|---|
| Subsidiaries include | Pella International, Inc., Pella, Iowa<br>Pella Product, Inc., Rockford, Illinois<br>Pella Windows & Doors, Inc., Glendale Heights, Illinois<br>Pella International Sales Corporation, Pella, Iowa<br>Pella Windows & Doors, Inc., Minneapolis, Minnesota<br>Viking Industries, Inc., Portland, Oregon<br>Cole Sewell, Minneapolis, Minnesota | |
| ADDRESS | 102 Main Street, Pella IA 50219<br>Phone: 515–628–1000<br><br>URL: http://www.pella.com | |
| BUSINESS | Fenestration products | |
| STATISTICS | Employees | 4,000 |
| | Other facts | Privately owned company controlled by the Kuper-Farver family. |

quently, Pella's management embarked on a major rejuvenation that would ultimately change every part of its business.

Like most old-line manufacturers, Pella's success and strengths were grounded in making good product. According to former senior vice president Hilliard Keeney, "Our philosophy was, if you built a better product, then somebody would come buy it."[4] Until 1992, Pella was selling entirely through independent distributors whose only window and patio door line was Pella, typically representing around 90 percent of their total sales. These distributors, who number about eighty today, performed many important functions including physical distribution, assembly (adding attachments and options and customizing product), and selling—which involved, among other activities, operating window stores to help customers effectively navigate the vast array of products, features, and options. Pella distributors experienced considerable cost to sell and ready the product for application. In addition, since the distributors handled almost all the marketing and sales, Pella itself had very limited insight into the market and customers, and to compound the problem, even basic industry data was sorely lacking.

## Market Understanding and Customer Segmentation

Pella's first action was to build a better understanding of what was happening in the market. It was apparent that the middle market was growing very rapidly. This was the portion of the market that was being driven by large increases in repair and remodeling (R&R) including the do-it-yourself and buy-it-yourself segments. The explosive growth of the home center channel, led by The Home Depot, Lowe's, and Menard's, was helping satisfy this demand and helping national manufacturers take share from local mill shops that built windows. Andersen, in particular, was a beneficiary of this middle market growth and had become the largest and fastest-growing national wood window maker. Pella, with its high-end product, exclusive distributors, and high-cost value chain, was focused on the premium end of the market, which was attractive but would not provide the long-term growth Pella needed and was positioned for.

Channel Champions: Windows by Pella (continued)

The answer for Pella was clear and was basically threefold:

- Drastically improve cost and service through the existing channel to serve the high-end segments of the market
- Capture growth opportunities in the middle segments of the market
- Drive brand development

Certainly one large hurdle for Pella was accepting that there was enormous opportunity to improve costs and service levels throughout its existing value chain. But the biggest mind-set change was the idea that Pella had to stop thinking about its distributors as its customers. Instead, regardless of its distributors' positions and desires, Pella had to take responsibility for marketing—understand the different end customer segments and then determine how the entire value chain could best serve them.

Crucial to this mind-set change was the concept of market segmentation. Traditional cuts of the market primarily captured distinctions between residential versus commercial and multifamily dwelling customers and between new and R&R construction. However, distinctions between customers within these categories had to be made in order to fully understand their various needs and determine how to best satisfy them. As a proxy for these different needs-based segments, Pella adopted a price (average dollars per window) segmentation. For example, $50 to $100 might be one segment at the low end and $200+ a high-end segment. Pella systematically assessed the differences across these segments and used that insight to rigorously distinguish what it offers to each segment, building very distinct value propositions (products and services) accordingly.

As Pella CEO Gary Christensen explains: "the concept of market segmentation was key and was extremely difficult because it was not the simple, traditional view of the business. It highlighted starkly different buying behaviors grouped around price points. We had to get past the conventional 'everything for everybody' perspective and have something practical that everyone in the company could use to define different solutions for different segments."[5]

## Market Segment–Focused Business Systems

Determining the basic strategic vision was the easy part; as is typical, getting there proved to be the real challenge. It entailed a long, arduous journey that, in fact, is still under way today. The changes encompassed every aspect of the business from products to manufacturing processes to channels and logistics to selling and marketing. Most notably, multiple business systems had to be developed to satisfy specific customer segments.

To successfully reach the middle market served by retailers and lumberyards, Pella had to build a completely separate business system. First, it had to design a new product line that could compete effectively against Andersen—one that would meet the quality and craftsmanship standards of Pella but would be more focused and therefore less costly than the traditional high-end products. This new product line with its separate sub-brand, ProLine, has a limited number of SKUs in contrast to Pella's historical build-to-order Designer Series product line that provides a virtually unlimited number of combinations of products, options, and configurations. The new ProLine product required completely different plants with radically different manufacturing processes, resources, and performance requirements in order to avoid the complexity and accompanying higher cost of the Designer Series.

The ProLine product is also sold direct to retailers, selected lumberyards, and specialty building material suppliers, requiring separate marketing, selling, and distribution processes. For instance, the logistics of restocking a large home center for the weekend rush have proven immensely different from those of fulfilling multiple custom homebuilders' orders. With the Designer Series, the homeowners will typically spend hours with a salesperson including visits to the Pella Window Store and meetings at the job site, ultimately stepping through 280 separate specifications that will determine the final product configuration. Key to customer satisfaction in this channel is Pella's taking a total project management approach. By contrast, the home center shopper must answer only about a dozen questions to place an order. Of course, Pella must also provide tailored sales and merchandizing support to the home centers. Customer satisfaction in this channel is based on supporting the unique transaction-selling environment of home centers, which drives substantive differences in order acquisition and fulfillment.

So, with the benefit of its segmentation insights, Pella was able to develop value propositions (products and services at the right cost and price) and the requisite separate business systems precisely targeted and optimized for specific customer segments.

## Major Business Improvements

Every aspect of the value chain was examined and almost nothing left unchanged.

- More responsive and lower-cost manufacturing
- Upgraded inventory and logistics for improved delivery reliability and lower cost
- New capabilities in channel service
- Redesigned systems to support these new capabilities.

Pella substantively improved its own cost, lead times, and reliability. Additionally, much of the value-added work previously performed by distributors was relocated back to Pella plants, resulting in further efficiencies.

A key factor in improving the value proposition in all channels was the upgrading of Pella's logistics capabilities. To ensure delivery reliability, Pella had to revamp its strategy. It was determined that the optimal model was a national distribution center serving home centers and distributors on a direct basis. In addition, investments in new information systems and re-engineered processes helped reduce response time and raise reliability and quality.

To make all this change happen, Pella had to rely on new management practices. The changes were too far-reaching and the implementation too involved to simply be mandated from top management. The devil was certainly in the detail. Thousands of small changes and subsequent refinements had to be made. They could only be made in a timely, cost-effective manner by people close to and knowledgeable about the issues—people given the latitude to actually implement improvements. The entire company was mobilized for the transformation. Pella has relied heavily on a Kaizen system for continuous improvement. Employees from management down to the shop floor were put on teams to address pressing issues. These teams were empowered to diagnose and address any problems or opportunities they found. This continuous improvement philosophy has been a critical element of Pella's progress. "Continuous Improvement using Kaizen has become a major part of our culture," says Christensen. "We tell each team to be action-oriented and avoid holding out for the perfect solution. We simply ask them to make it significantly better, knowing we'll come back to improve the process time and time again. And this isn't just for the plants. We use teams in every process in the business including the entire value chain. It is a remarkable thing to see."

## Brand Development

Within the fragmented collection of window manufacturers, only Pella and Andersen had established significant brand awareness at the consumer level. Andersen had initiated a sustained corporate brand-building program in the 1980s while Pella had relied on its distributors' local advertising and marketing programs. Going forward, it was clear to Pella's management that it would be important to take ownership of its brand development to fully leverage the significant changes and improvements from its segment-specific business strategy, its operational realignments, and its expanded access through new channels.

Fundamental to its brand strategy was that all Pella products would meet the same meticulous level of quality and performance that had become the hallmark of the Pella brand, regardless of the product or market segment to be served. An umbrella positioning statement for the Pella brand, "Viewed To Be The Best" was developed along with a common warranty for all products.

## Results and Conclusions

Since its recognition of a problem in the 1980s, Pella has undergone a true transformation that has yielded tremendous results. As Christensen describes it, "Today, compared to 1990, you will spend less money for a better Pella product and get it faster. Customer satisfaction is at an all-time high and continuing to improve." In fact, cycle times are one-third previous levels. The

Channel Champions: Windows by Pella (continued)

on-time delivery rate has gone from about 85 percent to 99 percent. There has been a tenfold improvement in inventory turns. On top of this, Pella has not had a significant price increase since 1993. Finally, sales more than doubled from 1991 to 1998, with growth coming from all segments. ProLine has not cannibalized other products, as some feared, even though it has grown tremendously. In fact, taken by itself, ProLine would place in the top fifteen North American companies in terms of wood window sales.

Christensen points out that only a small part of Pella's success can be attributed to the strategy—the bulk of the success has come from the execution. "If strategy is the front wheel of the bicycle, then implementation and continuous improvement are the back wheel that provides the power. Ninety percent of the work is getting it right."

He credits the continuous improvement culture using the Kaizen methodology for making the segment-focused business system approach work. This capability that Pella has established will be used in the years to come as Pella further understands the market and builds additional tailored business systems to serve targeted segments.

However, Christensen believes there is still a long way to go: "We're only 20 percent of the way there." The battle to maintain its successful customer segmentation strategy remains today. "The biggest risk we face is the tendency both inside and outside of the business to revert to the old unstructured 'all things to all people' approach. The world is no longer 'one size fits all.' Serving customers in lumberyards is different from home centers, which are different from window stores," notes Christensen. Interestingly, few building products manufacturers and retailers fully appreciate the importance and power of customer-focused business systems. Nonetheless, Pella is determined to continue to pursue its course. "In everything we do, we think about customer segments. We're letting customers drive the business," says Randy Iles, senior vice president marketing and sales.

*Channels by Pella*

- Market understanding and customer segmentation
- Market segment–focused business systems

# Section Three

# Channel Challenges

No one ever said it would be easy. Three things need to be borne in mind during the five-step channel management process:

1. *Managing Channel Conflict*

Achieving customer insight, identifying value-adding customer segments, and developing operating systems aligned to customers are the heart of the channel management process. Their transformation into effective channel management can be marred and confused by conflicts between channels. Multiple channels are an inherent part of channel management, which makes it inevitable that differences will arise between channels. Companies need to be increasingly adept at recognizing potential channel conflicts and making conscious trade-offs or investing in the capabilities to manage the conflict.

2. *Maximizing Channel Economics*

To stay ahead of the game, companies must proactively drive the changes. Channels are the new battleground and will be constantly changing. Only companies that match or exceed this tempo of change will survive. The winners of the future will be the companies brave enough and insightful enough to consistently invent new channels and manage them vigorously.

3.    *The One-to-One Advantage*

The end result of dynamic channel management is one-to-one marketing. Segments of one are the future. The beauty of e-commerce is simply that it allows for an intimate two-way conversation with your customers. Don't get carried away: the Internet is a great tool by which to achieve channel advantage—but not the only tool or the last word.

# Chapter 8
# Managing Channel Conflict

Honest differences are often a healthy sign of progress.
    —Mahatma Gandhi[1]

Business life is more complicated than the single question of which channels to select.

Many manufacturers currently face the issue of managing multiple, overlapping channels. Separate channels are essential if a company is to reach fragmenting customer segments, and the inevitable conflict among these channels must be managed.

The channel conflict questions usually have broad strategic implications and require systems investments to gain competitive advantage and resolve conflicts through managing information. In addition, they are often linked to near-term tactical and operational improvement opportunities, which can pay for building the capabilities.

Paint manufacturer Sherwin-Williams serves multiple channels and is adept at managing cross-channel conflict. It has to be. Sherwin-Williams paint flows through several different channels—mass merchant, home centers, independent paint stores, and Sherwin-Williams paint stores. The product itself is often similar, if not virtually the same; however, to serve a wide variety of customers, the brand name, the price, and the accompanying services and support all vary across channels and sometimes within a channel. The Sherwin-Williams United Coatings subsidiary makes Wal-Mart's Color Place line. Sherwin-Williams also makes the Martha Stewart line of designer paints for K-mart (though the Sherwin-Williams name is not on the can) and its Dutch Boy brand.[2] Sherwin-Williams's successful management of multiple channels is no longer an exception.

Frequently, tailoring products to a particular segment means offering not just a range of product options but also a range of channel options. The same product can be sold through dramatically different channels. In most markets multiple channels economically coexist. This shows that consumers differ in terms of their expectations about the purchase and ownership experience, as well as their expectations about the product. After all, a person can fit into multiple segments. You may visit a restaurant in a number of different roles—eating with your family, with colleagues, by yourself. On each occasion you will have different expectations and service demands.

Conflict is an inherent part of channel management. For any reasonably sized business it is virtually inevitable in one form or another. The reality is that purchasing or ownership-based segmentation frequently leads manufacturers to sell similar products through more than one channel. Obviously, this can—and does—lead to clashes.

Sometimes, conflicts between manufacturer and retailer are unavoidable. Take, for example, the car industry. The nature of the product is such (big ticket, infrequent purchase, easy to compare prices across retailers) that most consumers are highly price sensitive at the point of purchase and typically have a large number of same-make dealers relatively nearby to choose from. Therefore, the dealers' profit margins on new car sales are inevitably competed down to almost nothing. Dealers instead make their money from used car sales and service. This sets up a conflict of objectives: the manufacturer wants to sell new cars, the dealers want to sell used cars and service. Lexus helped address this problem by showing dealers how to manage the new and used car businesses together in ways that maximize the value of both (essentially, by increasing the residual value of its cars).

Conflict often breaks out when a supplier recognizes that existing channels are not performing satisfactorily—for example, not capturing the full or desired market share. The supplier tries to drive change in those channels or find new channels, but it often turns out that some of the existing channel members are unwilling or unable to make the necessary transition. (For example, new or alternative formats often attract new customers, but existing outlets may not have the space or resources to adopt them.) And, contrary to conventional wisdom, the answer is not always a channel partnership approach.

The extent of the conflict is largely determined by how much the underlying channel economics have shifted. The shift in economics over time corresponds to a supplier–channel relationship life cycle, which is comparable to a product life cycle. In the first stage, the interests of the two parties appear aligned as they rapidly grow the business. In this stage, conflict seldom exists and there is little need for adjusting the channel's behavior.

In the second stage, the need arises either to extract broad efficiency gains from the supplier–channel business system or to target customer satisfaction improvements or cost reductions, or both, for specific customer segments or channels.

In the third and final stage, either because the underlying economics have shifted so significantly or because the business is shrinking, the interests of the two parties are no longer aligned. Conflict can be intense and rampant. The supplier seeks to fundamentally redesign ways to serve the customer. Often entirely new business systems must be established.

Indeed, the third stage often provides an ideal opportunity for a new participant in the market.

# Minimizing Conflict; Maximizing Difference

The classic ways of managing conflict across channels all have to do with minimizing competition between the different channels by differentiating their offers from each other as much as possible. This can be achieved through variations in product ranges, brand names, pricing strategies, and advertising and promotional programs.

With the increasing fragmentation of end markets, most suppliers are finding that it is more and more difficult to use just one channel to access their total potential market and to grow. Thus they must confront the challenge of managing the conflicts across multiple channels so as to maximize customer reach and satisfaction.

These conflicts have two root causes. One is pricing and incentive differences. The other is competition for the same customers.

The pricing issues must be viewed comprehensively to prevent arbitrage across channels and across levels in the distribution hierarchy, to keep one channel from dominating other important channels and to ensure that required value-added services can be supported by the appropriate channels. Some level of competition for customers among channels may be desired, but any damaging overlap should be identified in the planning stage.

The arsenal that suppliers can draw upon to manage these potential conflicts and to serve the various needs of different customers and different channels is extensive—brand differences, product differences, supplier-provided service differences, incentive and price policy, upfront allocation of customer types, supply policy, or order size differences. Adroitly designing and deploying the appropriate mix of tactics to achieve a desired end game is crucial to protecting existing markets and to securing new ones.

# Organize Around Channels

Managing channel conflict is also an operations and structural issue. It is imperative for management to ensure that companies are organized and managed in such a way that they connect with customers—the right customers, at the right time, in the right way. Managing conflict is an organizational issue as much as anything.

This means that customer service can't be delegated, passed down the line. Delegating customer care improvement to a customer service function is a sure sign that the results will be disappointing. In fact, delegating responsibility down into any functional organization without significant senior management attention and forethought seldom works well.

Connecting with customers does not mean smiling at them—though that helps. It means creating channels that provide customers with value and then creating the operational systems and processes to deliver that value effectively. The operational challenge is a broad one. The business processes relevant to efficient management of a particular channel invariably involve several functional areas. Sales, marketing, operations, and financial interests need to be considered. Strategic, operational, and information system skills are required.

The challenge is for companies to perceive the impact that organizing their activities around channels rather than functions would have on their effectiveness. For start-ups this is plainly easier—as witnessed by Saturn and Lexus. They can work backward from the channel to create the operational systems that maintain it effectively.

## Channel Champions: Goodyear

A particularly difficult issue is how to move from single-channel to multiple-channel distribution. While there is no painless way to achieve this feat, lessons can be learned from the experiences of manufacturers that have done so.

For example, the tire industry has a wide range of channels. There are multibrand suppliers, discount stores, single brand suppliers, service stations, and companies such as Sears, as well as warehouse clubs. Purchase experiences are different and customer expectations of purchase experiences are also different. There are channel-specific brands and ranges of prices between channels. Not surprisingly, tire companies are used to dealing with channel conflict.

Faced with such a marketplace, companies must ask, Who controls the customer relationship? And, How much influence do they want over the customer relationship?

The answers aren't easy. Ask Goodyear.

Goodyear is a major designer, manufacturer, and distributor of tires and related products. In 1998 Goodyear had over 95,000

| COMPANY | Goodyear Tire & Rubber Company | |
|---|---|---|
| ADDRESS | 1144 E. Market Street, Akron OH 44316–0001, USA<br>Phone: 330–796–2121   Fax: 330–796–2222<br><br>URL: www.goodyear.com | |
| BUSINESS | Rubber and plastic products | |
| STATISTICS | Employees | 1997   95,472 |
| | Annual sales (mil) | 1998   $12,626 |
| | Annual results<br>Net income (mil) | 1998   $682 |
| | Other facts | #1 truck and tire manufac-<br>turer in the United States;<br>#3 in the world |

employees, market capitalization of $8 billion, revenue of $12.6 billion, and profits of $682.3 million.

Retail tire distribution channels are differentiated primarily along the dimension of exclusivity. At opposite ends of the spectrum are a pure brand exclusive channel (single brand of product, high control of the channel, and high service offerings) and a multibrand channel (broad product selection, very low prices, low service, and high volume). Goodyear's distribution channel today is a mix of exclusive and multibrand, balancing the control and price realization of the exclusive channel and the volume and competitive nature of the multibrand channel.

The late eighties saw a number of undesirable trends occurring at Goodyear. Its replacement tire shipments declined from 18.9 million units in 1986 to 16.2 million in 1989. In addition, Goodyear's share of tires on new car shipments declined from 12.8 percent to 10.5 percent from 1986 to 1989. Profits from replacement tires were also heading downward at the same time. In 1990, Goodyear incurred a net loss of $38 million on revenues of $11 billion.

In some presumably exclusive dealerships, Goodyear tires were stacked next to those with lesser-known brand names but higher profit margins. Michelin was meanwhile plunging ahead, selling to anyone. The exclusivity associated with the Goodyear brand was threatened: at least 35 percent of Goodyear dealers sold other brands of tires, and 35 to 45 percent of Goodyear's replacement volume was sold through multibrand dealerships.

Examination of the market prompted a number of important insights. First, consumers can be segmented by whether they base tire purchases primarily on the brand, the distribution outlet, or the price. Clearly, Goodyear's strength lay in the first group.

The second insight was that Goodyear's retail stores were experiencing inefficiencies at both the operational and administrative level. The retail stores' SG&A as a percentage of revenue was significantly higher than at most of Goodyear's competitors.

The conclusion from this was that Goodyear should enhance its mix of exclusive and multibrand distribution. The exclusive format could be economically viable, and the increased earnings resulting from growing the channel and strengthening Goodyear's brand equity would be well worth the investment.

There were also opportunities for improving the efficiency of the retail stores in several areas, including purchasing, staffing schedules, organization, and staff incentive programs. Furthermore, an opportunity for head count reduction provided a means of bringing the retail stores' SG&A into line with that of Goodyear's competitors.

Goodyear developed a three-year implementation plan for the new approach.

The first step involved increasing the numbers of retail distribution outlets to more effectively penetrate Goodyear's markets. This was enabled by a new distribution site development process and supporting analysis, with emphasis on achieving more economically viable channel outlets.

Goodyear then restructured its logistics network to achieve same-day or next-day capability for 60 percent of the market, better inventory management, and multimillion-dollar cost savings.

The next step was to increase Goodyear advertising on both its products and the outlets that sold them, so as to further strengthen brand equity. The company then identified and implemented other profit enhancement opportunities for its owned retail stores, over and above the increased advertising.

As the last step of the plan, Goodyear began explicitly selling tires into specific multibrand outlets such as Sears with an edited selection. It also developed a new format called Just Tires, whose outlets focused exclusively on selling tires rather than combining tire sales with other routine maintenance services.

Goodyear's most recent initiative is an alliance with its Japanese competitor, Sumitomo Rubber. With total 1997 sales of $4.7 billion, Sumitomo has rights to the Dunlop brand in major world markets. The alliance was aimed at achieving savings of $300 to $360 million. In addition, it combined Sumitomo's strength in Japan with Goodyear's strength in North America and Europe. The new combination boasts 22.6 percent of the $69.5 billion world tire market, making it the leading player—Bridgestone manages 18.6 percent, narrowly ahead of Michelin's 18.3 percent.[3] Whether the alliance will solve Goodyear's problems is debatable, but it does provide access to a range of products that expands Goodyear's channel options and, as Charles Goodyear demonstrated, hope can spring eternal.

*Channels by Goodyear*

- Understand customer segments based on differences in purchase behavior.
- Win in multiple customer segments with different channels and formats.
- Use analytical tactical marketing (for example, new site development) for successful roll-out.
- Focus on operational improvements that enhance value.

## Channel Champions: How GE Smooths Conflict

General Electric's Appliance Division is one of the leading U.S. manufacturers of "white goods"—refrigerators, freezers, ranges, cooktops, wall ovens, dishwashers, washing machines. GE Appliances sells over 10 million appliances in 150 world markets. Its brands include Monogram, GE Profile, Hotpoint, and RCA.

In the mid-1980s, GE had strong U.S. share positions in three of the five major appliance categories—refrigerators, ranges, and dishwashers. Furthermore, from a distribution channel standpoint, GE held the leadership position in the building contractor and independent retailer distribution segments, which together repre-

| COMPANY | **General Electric Company** | |
|---|---|---|
| Subsidiaries include | National Broadcasting Company, Inc. GE Capital Services GE Aircraft Engines | |
| ADDRESS | 3135 Easton Turnpike, Fairfield CT 06431–0001 USA Phone: 203–373–2211   Fax: 203–373–3497  URL: http://www.ge.com | |
| BUSINESS | Electronics, electrical equipment, lighting, power, medical devices, plastics, financial services . . . | |
| STATISTICS | Employees | 1997    276,000 |
| | Annual sales (mil) | 1998    $100,469 |
| | Annual results Net income (mil) | 1998    $9,296 |
| | Other facts | GE is the only company listed in the Dow Jones Industrial Index today that was also included in the original 1896 index; GE topped *Fortune's* survey of America's most admired companies both in 1998 and 1999. |

sented 47 percent of the market. GE was much weaker in the mass merchandiser and megadealer segments, which dominated the remaining 53 percent of the market.

Unfortunately for GE, the U.S. retail industry for appliances and consumer electronics was changing dramatically. The mass merchandisers and megadealers were successfully targeting a segment of consumers looking for basic products at the lowest possible prices. In consumer electronics, or "brown goods," GE had emphasized these new channels in an attempt to build volume, only to see margins and brand loyalty erode. The large dealers were using their buying power to negotiate lower and lower prices from manufacturers. Furthermore, these dealers wished to maintain their low-price image and resisted selling the manufacturers' most profitable high-end product lines. As a group, independent distributors, unable to compete with the scale advantages of the megadealers and mass merchandisers, came under severe earnings pressure, and many went out of business.

GE exited this business and was determined to prevent a similar occurrence in the white goods business.

As part of a concerted effort to establish a course of action, GE explored in some depth the changing channel and consumer demands. For instance, GE tapped into its customer service help desk, the GE Answer Center, to help gather valuable market research on evolving product and service preferences. In addition, it spent time exploring consumer and channel needs and behaviors through other primary research methods.

GE found that the service and product offerings across channel segments were indeed quite different, and these channel segments in turn naturally aligned with the needs of different consumer segments of the market. In particular, GE ascertained that a large segment of consumers did value the service, relationship, and higher-end product selection of the independent appliance dealer and contractor channels. If GE could find a way to bolster the economics of the independent channels against the onslaught of the mass merchandisers and megadealers, then the manufacturer could satisfy this profitable consumer segment and prevent a repeat of the brown goods story.

In building its understanding of consumers and channels, GE found that the manufacturer-supplied support and services

Channel Champions: How GE Smooths Conflict (continued)

required by the independent dealers differed substantially from those required by the larger channel players. One of the most critical differences was in the demand pattern placed on the distribution network. For example, megadealers who were replenishing sizable inventories desired full truckloads of product on a predictable schedule, whereas the independents had more erratic demand requiring smaller shipments and more rapid response. Small dealers and building contractors could not afford to carry large inventories. Therefore, they were forced to limit their product offering, provide uneven delivery time performance to consumers, and rely more heavily on the manufacturers' ability to deliver small (at times single-item) orders in a timely manner.

Other examples of differences in services required:

- Building contractors needed twenty-four-hour access to product dimensions and blueprints from their building sites.
- Small retailers needed general business planning assistance, something large dealers could afford to do for themselves.
- Independent retailers needed easy, fast access to manufacturers' product information so they could offer consumers superior product knowledge, a key competitor differentiator for this channel.

GE initiated a two-pronged strategy:

- Broaden the product offering in major appliances to effectively meet the needs of price-conscious consumers served well by the megadealer and mass merchandiser channels. Goal: continue to improve sales through these growing channels without jeopardizing the leadership position in the other channels.
- Restructure systems, processes, and organization to better serve the smaller channel players, and to improve their economics. In particular, build a distribution capability to meet the demand patterns of these channel customers and reduce their logistics costs. Goal: create a sustainable competitive advantage and continue to profitably reach the large traditional consumer segment served by these channels.

The distribution opportunities were addressed through fundamental changes to GE's physical distribution system whereby GE now offers fast response, high availability for small volume, local supply. GE had to build and employ a low-cost, cross-docking approach to distributing product. This delivery service was complemented by the development of a manufacturer-direct ordering system called Premier Plus. As a result, retailers are able to place orders for products directly into GE's inventory and production planning system and receive their shipments the next day. This system allows the small retailers to effectively shift their inventories to GE, reducing the retailer's costs. The dealers were, in turn, able to sell and display a larger variety of GE's offering, including the high-end products. Another benefit to GE was that since the Premier Plus orders represented actual demand rather than shipments to dealers' inventories, GE was able to improve production planning and hence reduce factory inventory costs as well. Overall, GE is reported to have reduced distribution and marketing costs to these dealers by over 10 percent.

In addition to this logistics system, GE created other services as part of the program targeted primarily to small businesses. Member retailers have access to business revitalization loans, store remodeling kits, and business management software. Also included is the ability of the retailer to source business equipment, computer software, and telephone services at GE's negotiated lower rates. However, these elements of the program are valued much less by the channel than the logistics and ordering system.

In many cases, in exchange for participation in the program, GE obtains commitments from the participants such as share of business, volume, and breadth of product coverage granted to GE.

As a result of these efforts, GE has maintained a leading position in the independent retailer and building contractor segments, which still constitute about 40 percent of the market. Independent retailers consistently praise GE's efforts. According to one retailer, "GE absolutely does an excellent job of providing services," and another maintains "GE bends over backwards to help satisfy the customer." The independents have been able to hold their own against mass merchandisers, with instances of individual retailers reporting increased profit margins of up to 3 percent and substantial increases in volume. GE was able to fill special orders within a

Channel Champions: How GE Smooths Conflict (continued)

day while competitors often took four or five days. Perhaps most notably, the success of GE's efforts has generated substantial end customer value. The consumers seeking the service and product selection of the smaller channel players still have that option, and the delivery service and product selection available to them has greatly improved.

GE has also grown its share of the megadealer channel and as a result holds the number two share position in this segment. GE is estimated to hold the number two share position in the retail department store channel—primarily consisting of Sears—as well. In the process of growing its share position in this highly competitive industry, GE has returned the division to its historical profitability levels, with an operating margin of 11 percent, up from the roughly 8 percent margins in the late 1980s.

*Channels from GE*

- Recognize and support the economic viability of traditional channels.
- Own the face to the customer—customer service, repairs, delivery.
- Leverage multiple brands and models across distribution channels to minimize conflict.

## Taking GE on the Road

So robust is GE and Jack Welch's approach that it could be potentially transferred into many other industries. Once you realize that products aren't everything and bundling the right services to the right people at the right time is more important, things take on new perspectives.

What if, for example, GE decided to shake things up in the automotive industry?

As Jack Welch analyzed the automotive industry he would see an attractive opportunity to increase shareholder value using approaches honed at GE. His strategy would have two basic elements: profitable growth through services and major cost reduction.

As with his medical devices, aircraft engine, and other businesses he would view the automotive market largely as a mature engineered-product market with vast potential for growth through services. He has lamented that a mere 60 percent of GE's profits come from services and expressed a wish for it to be 80 percent.[4] In the automotive industry, we believe Welch would identify the best opportunity as downstream services. He would seek to leverage the strong credit, superior financial services capabilities, and leading innovation that have made GE Capital the primary growth engine for GE. He would want to reap the rewards of reshaping the industry without making any physical product.

Welch would also see enormous opportunities to reduce costs and enhance quality in downstream activities. He would fully recognize that an inordinate amount of cost is added to a vehicle past the factory gate because of an inefficient, outdated dealer channel, misaligned OE and dealer incentives, and suboptimal operating practices. In addition, he would pick up on the level of discontent customers have with the dealer experience and the importance of true customer satisfaction. As at GE, he would see that improving the quality of downstream operations is key to cutting costs. He would establish goals for drastic improvements and motivate capable managers to meet them.

Dreamland? Perhaps, but think of Jack Welch's excellent base. GE's Auto Financial Services unit already provides leasing, insurance, and financial products to end customers. This unit also sells dealers a variety of financial services including inventory,

## Taking GE on the Road (continued)

commercial, and rental car financing. In addition, GE Capital Fleet Services is the largest fleet management company in the world, providing a variety of services beyond leases: maintenance programs, accident prevention programs, programs for tracking fuel consumption, best practice sharing, and resale management.

Welch could embark on a mission to expand these positions to become the number one provider of sales and after-sales support, beginning in the United States and then spreading into Europe, followed by other parts of the world. He would expect to fundamentally alter the downstream portion of the value chain and then use his clout to drive improvements back up the value chain. This would be accomplished through three thrusts.

In the first, Welch expands the business of selling financial services to dealers and begins supplying most of the services a dealer needs to operate. He uses this capability to provide outsourcing of dealer operations at lower cost than the dealers can realize themselves. In addition, he aggressively acquires his own set of dealers. His competitive advantages come from applying best practices, economies of scale, and rationalizing his growing network of owned and operated dealers to reduce costs and improve customer service.

Second, he continues to grow his fleet management business, enlarging its scope to offer full-service leasing for any type of business account. He can manage all aspects of vehicle ownership for new and used vehicles. He offers a wide variety of financing and leasing plans that effectively allow him to sell mobility service to business customers or to even operate the fleet for the customer. He employs best practices, superior information and experience, and scale to provide these services at a lower cost than the customers can achieve for themselves and lower cost than they can get from his competitors.

Third, he strives to radically change the car ownership paradigm for consumers. Instead of focusing on selling cars, he offers to sell consumers mobility contracts where consumers pay a regular payment that includes vehicle usage, insurance, maintenance, and other tailored services. He provides a wide variety of programs customized to an individual consumer's needs and interests. For instance, an individual's mobility contract could contain rapid, comprehensive roadside assistance for the safety-minded or advanced driving courses for the driving enthusiast. Innovative new services are also continuously developed to sell to end customers. He builds on existing consumer credit information technology and management capabilities to collect in-depth information about car-buyers' needs and behaviors. This information is used to market mobility to consumers and to manage their mobility experience more efficiently and effectively than traditional methods. For example, he is able to provide a variety of customized replacement options for consumers whose mobility contracts are expiring, getting in touch with them before expiration and with attractive incentives for moving to a new contract early. In this way demand becomes much easier to forecast and thus manage.

Furthermore, he becomes quite adept at maximizing the value of a vehicle over its entire life cycle. The option of retaining ownership of a vehicle over its entire useful life allows the asset's value to be better managed. He can optimize new and retained values through careful, integrated management of a variety of programs: warranties, maintenance programs, usage monitoring, mobility contracts of different types and lengths, contracted retained value incentives and disincentives for consumers, rental programs, fleet turnover, inventory, and used car sales—all on a national or global scale.

To accomplish his bold vision GE takes positions in not just dealerships but also other service providers as needed to secure a leading position and to be able to control all the service elements needed at the lowest possible cost. For example, some of these acquisitions include service and repair networks, other leasing companies, used car auction companies, rental car companies, and fleet management systems providers.

As has been his hallmark at GE, Jack Welch pursues his vision relentlessly. He sets extraordinarily high goals for his managers, and his expectations are even higher. Not meeting his aggressive targets is simply unacceptable. He demands and achieves huge, simultaneous growth in margins, market share, and quality. The speed at which he makes progress is surprising to the whole industry, particularly since he insists on both short- and long-term performance gains: "You can't grow long term if you can't eat short term."[5]

## Taking GE on the Road (continued)

As GE's ambitions are increasingly fulfilled downstream, Welch's power is wielded to change the game upstream, and the vehicle manufacturers and their suppliers are forced to bend to his will. His leading share of sales and service in the U.S. market affords him substantial influence with the OEs. Jack also has vastly superior information about consumer needs and wants. Consequently, he begins to dictate vehicle design requirements to the OEs.

He projects his disdain for bureaucracy and insists on massive cuts in OE sales, marketing, and service functions since he does not need this support from the OEs, having built the needed capabilities himself. As he develops greater abilities to forecast and control consumer demand through his various customer and asset life cycle management programs, he provides OEs improved forecasts—but in return insists both on reduced supply chain costs to be reflected in prices and on shorter response times.

He uses his market power in the parts business, suppressing OE parts margins and in some cases dealing directly with the OEs' vendors or alternative suppliers to secure better prices and support. Additionally, Welch understands that for many vehicles, consumers' downstream experience has a greater effect on satisfaction levels and loyalty than the manufacturer-controlled variables (for example, the vehicle design). This fact combined with his operation's size allow him to begin to insist that OEs bid for the privilege of supplying his sales and service business. For his portfolio he carefully picks and chooses the best models from various manufacturers. As a result, the manufacturers' brand equity is reduced while his is increased, competitive pressures on the manufacturers are heightened, and further restructuring and consolidation takes place upstream.

Not surprisingly, in this story OEs and their suppliers rue the day that Jack Welch evaluated the automotive value chain and embarked on a mission to fundamentally improve it by leveraging services and reducing costs downstream.

Is this scenario dreamland? If so, what type of dream is it? Pure fantasy, nightmare, or a dream that can come true? Many people in the automotive industry are truly concerned about the potential for powerful new channels to arise in the wake of rapid channel evolution. Major channel conflicts are already on the horizon.

## Channel Champions: The Direct Route

Some of the most notable business successes of recent years have come from companies creating new channels.

Nowhere is this more true than in financial services. First Direct (now part of the Hong Kong Shanghai Banking Corporation) was the first to offer telephone banking in the United Kingdom. First Direct is built around a simple question: What resources (human and technological) does it take to deliver a telephone banking channel? In response, the company created a new channel to reach young professionals who were often too busy to go into a bank branch during the day.

First Direct was launched in 1989 amid a blaze of publicity. An idiosyncratic, sometimes plain elusive, advertising campaign marked telephone banking's baptism into public consciousness. It was bold—First Direct set out to lead a banking revolution—and risky. People don't necessarily like an irreverent upstart, especially one dealing with their money.

First Direct has stuck to its telephones even though it took until 1994 for it to become profitable. Its advertising is now easier to fathom and a steady stream of customers are being converted to the pleasures of making direct debits at three o'clock in the morning. With 550,000 customers and an additional 10,000 a month joining, First Direct predicts it will have a million customers by the year 2000—not bad when you consider that most

| COMPANY | First Direct | |
|---|---|---|
| ADDRESS | Poultry, London, United Kingdom EC2P 2BX<br>Phone: 0171–260–800<br><br>URL: http://www.firstdirect.com | |
| BUSINESS | On-line banking | |
| | Other facts | Part of Midland Bank, which is owned by HSBC Holdings PLC. |

Channel Champions: The Direct Route (continued)

commentators envisaged First Direct as a small niche business rather than as a major player in financial services.

The customers are signing up to a bank that has no branches, accepting the phone lines as their major link with their money. "We are a bank which is remote from our customers. We are not tangible so all our communications—by telephone, mail or on the Internet—are direct. They are the way we do business," says First Direct's Peter Simpson. "Intelligent dialog with our customers replaces the traditional face-to-face relationship."[6]

First Direct has a factory and two buildings, one of which is the size of a generously apportioned football field. Costs are neatly contained and the savings passed on to customers. But it is not only a question of lower costs. The resulting organization is strikingly different in outlook from the traditional bank. "Our managers are trying to move away from a hierarchical form of management to one in which people at all levels understand their roles, and managers perform more of a coaching role than a supervisory one," says First Direct's chief executive, Kevin Newman, who thinks of employees directly serving customers as "profit generators" and the remainder as "those who will improve tomorrow's profit." Newman argues that in banking, the HR and IT functions are equally important. Investing in these, he says, is the main means of finding opportunities to save or cut costs and become more profitable. It is an argument that is only now beginning to appeal to traditional banks.

First Direct has shaken the traditional relationship between bank and customer. No more anxious meetings with the manager. Farewell to lines at the teller window. This is ironic when you consider that First Direct is actually a division of Midland Bank, in turn part of the mammoth HSBC. When it looked into the possibilities of telephone banking, Midland concluded that to succeed any organization would have to start from scratch. Transforming the Midland with its 1,500 branches into a telephone banking operation was a definite nonstarter.

Initial market research prior to the bank's launch suggested that four things would make it succeed—speed, convenience, value for money, and quality of service. "We realized that traditional areas of differentiation—having a great concept or a high quality product—would not be enough in themselves, because competitors can copy your ideas so quickly these days, and perhaps even do it better because they have a chance to learn from your mistakes," says Newman.

First Direct's selling point is being more responsive to customers than any other financial services organization. And research shows that it is perceived to have the highest quality of service of any banking organization in the United Kingdom. First Direct is almost evangelical in its fervor, words not normally associated with the banking fraternity. The acid test for First Direct's banking representatives is the "Moment of Truth"—on their hundredth phone call, at the end of a busy seven-hour shift, will they be committed enough to want to make this last customer feel special?

First Direct's success is partly built around the recognition that quality service is not simply about getting the mechanics right and doing what the customer requests, but also the way you go about it. Answering the telephone within three rings is a noble objective, but it's not much use if you can't provide assistance when you do answer. First Direct estimates that the banking representative who answers the phone is able to deal with 85 percent of requests and queries. As 98 percent of its staff have not worked for a bank before, they are unencumbered by notions of how things should—or used to—be done.

When it comes to people, First Direct is highly selective. Its brand of upbeat service is not for everyone. Says Kevin Newman: "We are recruiting against a set of criteria of which attitudes are not the least. Fundamentally, we want people who can relate to customers, who can listen, which is a pretty underrated skill, who probably have a level of aptitude in terms of numeracy, and are reasonably articulate. We think we can, with the investment we have made in computers, teach people the banking side of the operation. What we cannot teach people is the set of values, in the same way that we cannot force the culture on people."

Of course, First Direct's success has not gone unnoticed. Most of the big banks now offer a telebanking alternative to their traditional services and market researcher Mintel calculates that 20 percent of routine banking will done by telephone by the end of the decade.

## Channel Champions: The Direct Route (continued)

*Channels According to First Direct*

- Speed
- Convenience
- Value for money
- Quality of service
- Culture is built not bought

## Channel Champions: Organized to Deliver

Fundamental value enhancement requires coherency across functions. It also demands coherency across internal and external organizational boundaries and across decision-time horizons.

Channel issues are usually complex. Typically, numerous customer segments are involved, as are multiple channels performing several functions. Although channels should be dissected and assessed at the individual function level, they form a system with interconnected paths and linkages and these must also be analyzed and understood. Organized around channels, companies form networks.

W.W. Grainger was founded in 1927 when William W. Grainger recognized the need for an efficient wholesale electric motor sales organization that could provide customers with products faster than motor manufacturers could. He established a business in Chicago and generated sales through an eight-page catalog he called the Motor Book.

| COMPANY | W.W. Grainger, Inc. | |
|---|---|---|
| ADDRESS | 455 Knightsbridge Parkway, Lincolnshire IL 60069–3620 USA  Phone: 847–793–9030   Fax: 847–647–5669  URL: http://www.grainger.com | |
| BUSINESS | Wholesale—maintenance, repair, and operating supplies | |
| STATISTICS | Employees | 1997   15,299 |
| | Annual sales (mil) | 1998   $4,341 |
| | Annual results Net income (mil) | 1998   $238.5 |
| | Other facts | 70 percent of US businesses are within 20 minutes of a Grainger branch. |

Channel Champions: Organized to Deliver (continued)

Grainger is not and never has been in a sexy business. For example, it sells sump pumps and warehouse fans to small manufacturers, contractors, and distributors and is the leading distributor of maintenance, repair, and operating supplies and related information in North America.

W.W. Grainger was established to exploit service-based differentiation. The products were the same, but W.W. Grainger got them to the customer more quickly. Within six years, the company's reputation for service had grown sales to $250,000. Today, it has sales of over $4 billion (1997).

Grainger's ethos remains unchanged. It has over 1,500 full-time sales representatives; it has electronic databases that enable it to look up products by manufacturer's model number, brand name, description, or stock number; and it has a satellite network linking 350 local branches, two regional distribution centers, one national distribution center, and six zone distribution centers throughout all fifty states to ensure product availability.

As a result of this system, Grainger provides over 190,000 repair and replacement parts from over 550 suppliers. All are available twenty-four hours a day, seven days a week. Its network is such that 70 percent of U.S. businesses are within twenty minutes of a Grainger branch.

To Grainger the network is all.

It is significant that when the company moved into Canada it didn't slowly build up its presence, it bought an already established chain, Acklands (for $251.8 million in 1996), so that it had a ready-made network.

Grainger's resilience can be attributed to its willingness to continually seek out new channels and hone the channels it already uses. Its logistics systems, built around continuous replenishment, are continually enhanced.

Most recently Grainger has entered a collaboration with Perot Systems Corporation on the development of an Internet-based business-to-business commerce solution designed at improving the purchase of business supplies, equipment, and services. "At Grainger, we recognize that as technology advances, many customers will choose to purchase products through more innovative channels," says chairman and CEO Richard Keyser. The collaboration will create a one-stop shopping system and, it is hoped, streamline buying to small and medium-sized businesses.[7]

*Channels by Grainger*

- Differentiate your channel service.
- Continually learn and improve your channel model.

# Chapter 9
# Maximizing Channel Economics

Ideas are good for a limited time, not forever. The Internet and other new channels can fundamentally change the nature of the firm. You have to change the nature of the beast. A Tokyo Stock Company has invested $40 million to secure a two second advantage.

Traditional accounting laws of depreciation are irrelevant.
Orchestras have to transform themselves into jazz ensembles.
— Jeff Sampler, London Business School[1]

Channel champions revolutionize their industries.

AutoNation is revolutionizing automotive retailing with its used car superstores and, with its purchases of car rental companies, suggests that it is thinking of the life cycle management of cars. Wayne Huzinga has revolutionized waste management, video rentals, and now car retailing.

As the importance of service differentiation grows, new segments are unearthed, and purchasing and ownership segmentation becomes more sophisticated, the economics of many businesses are being radically altered.

There is more than one Michael Dell.

If change is to happen, new ways of thinking about the economics of the business are required. Companies must find opportunities to change the economics of the market by changing channels or realigning existing channels.

Think of the rapidly emerging channels in the music business. "Groups such as the Internet Underground Music Archive are posting digital audio tracks from unknown artists on the network, potentially subverting the role that record labels play," report Harvard Business School's Jeffrey Rayport and John Sviokla. "Today's technology allows musicians to record and edit material inexpensively themselves, and to distribute and promote it over networks such as the World Wide Web or commercial on-line services. They can also test consumers' reactions to their music, build an audience for their recorded performances, and distribute their products entirely in the marketspace."

The commercial logic is simple: "Bringing music to market can sometimes be done faster, better, and less expensively in the marketspace."[2]

Industry transformation is the order of the day. Strategy guru Gary Hamel, coauthor of *Competing for the Future,* argues that there are three kinds of companies. First are "the real makers," companies such as British Airways and Xerox. They are the aristocracy—well-managed, consistent high achievers. Second, says Hamel, are the takers, "peasants who only keep what the Lord doesn't want." This group typically have around 15 percent market share—such as Kodak in the copier business or Avis— "Avis' slogan *We try harder* enshrined the peasantry in its mission statement. Harder doesn't get you anywhere," says Hamel dismissively.[3]

Third are the breakers, industrial revolutionaries. These are companies Hamel believes are creating the new wealth—like Starbucks in the coffee business. "Companies should be asking themselves, who is going to capture the new wealth in your industry?" he says.

When Hamel talks of change, he is not considering tinkering at the edges. "The primary agenda is to be the architect of industry transformation not simply corporate transformation," he says. Companies that view change as an internal matter are liable to be left behind. Instead they need to look outside their industry boundaries. Hamel calculates that if you want to see the future coming, 80 percent of the learning will take place outside company and industry boundaries. This is not something companies are very good at. "The good news is that companies in most industries are blind in the same way," says Hamel.

"There is no inevitability about the future. There is no proprietary data about the future. The goal is to imagine what you can make happen."

And change will certainly happen. Markets can become victims of their own maturity. As markets mature, non–product-based differentiation tends to drive customer choice and relevant customer segment boundaries. The fundamental economics and basis of competition change. Power tends to flow downstream to the distribution channels who are creating the differentiation consumers value (and to the customers themselves). New power channels arise, posing major strategic and operational challenges for manufacturers. In any event, costs and effectiveness beyond the factory gate and beyond the manufacturer's company boundaries become ever more critical for growth and success.

# PC Channels

The PC industry has seen many dramatic changes in its relatively short history. Starting with technological innovation it has evolved through several phases to become a large, sophisticated industry with many types of players. Initially the PC industry was driven by new technology created by a few pioneers. They began by selling their rather crude products through direct channels—IBM had its direct sales staff, Apple sold computers direct to engineers who responded to magazine advertisements. In addition, the industry was quite vertically integrated by today's standards, making it difficult for more than a few companies to participate.

However, this situation quickly changed as the industry began to attract a wide variety of new entrants. They could rely on rapidly maturing sets of suppliers for virtually every portion of the PC, including most of the manufacturing value added. Also, as product quality and technology improved and as growing masses of customers became more comfortable with the product, a wealth of retail channels facilitated the broad expansion of the market. These channels, of course, were much less costly and had vastly greater reach than the direct sales models initially employed. Selling costs dropped from an average of 25 percent of industry revenue to 12 percent of revenue.

## The Belgian Movie Classic

In a 1997 *Harvard Business Review* article, W. Chan Kim and Renee Mauborgne—two academics from the French business school, INSEAD—outlined the findings from a five-year study.[4] They looked at thirty high-growth companies from around the world, and found that what distinguished them from less successful firms was the way they approached strategy.

This research gave rise to the theory of "value innovation"— something with important implications for channel management. In essence, what Chan Kim and Mauborgne suggest is that more successful companies reinvent the game rather than simply looking to get one step ahead.

As they explain, "The less successful companies took a conventional approach: their strategic thinking was dominated by the idea of staying ahead of the competition. In stark contrast, the high-growth companies paid little attention to matching or beating their rivals. Instead they sought to make competitors irrelevant through a strategic logic we call *value innovation*."

For example, Chan Kim and Mauborgne relate the story of Bert Claeys, a Belgian company that operates movie theaters. The Belgian movie theater business declined steadily from the 1960s to the 1980s. The spread of VCRs and satellite and cable television meant that the number of times an average Belgian went to see a movie in a year fell from eight to two.

By the early 1980s, many cinemas were forced to close down. Those that remained competed head-to-head for a shrinking market. All followed the same strategy, converting cinemas into multiplexes with up to ten screens. At the same time they broadened their film offerings to attract a wider range of customers, expanded their food and drink services, and increased the number of showings per day.

But in 1988, all of these efforts became irrelevant when Bert Claeys created Kinepolis—the world's first megaplex (basically, an enhanced channel for delivering the movie theater experience). With twenty-five screens and 7,600 seats, it offered moviegoers a radically superior service, and put the magic back into a night at the movies.

Other Belgian movie theaters, including multiplexes, for example, had small viewing rooms, screens measuring about seven meters by five meters, and 35-millimeter projection equipment. Viewing rooms at Kinepolis have up to seven hundred seats, including enough leg-room that viewers do not have to move when someone wants to pass. Bert Claeys installed oversized seats with individual armrests and designed the viewing space with a steep slope to ensure every customer had an unobstructed view.

At Kinepolis, screens measure up to twenty-nine meters by ten meters and rest on their own foundations so that sound vibrations are not transmitted from one screen to another. Many viewing rooms have 70-millimeter projection equipment and state-of-the-art sound equipment.

Kinepolis won 50 percent of the market in Brussels in its first year and expanded the market by about 40 percent. To gauge its impact, one need only listen—many Belgians no longer refer to a night at the movies but to an evening at Kinepolis.

The films as a product, of course, remained the same. But the experience of the moviegoer was enhanced through the creation of a new (or at least improved) channel. In the process, Bert Claeys also earned margins that were more than double the industry average.

## Channel Champions: The Daewoo Difference

Shaping new markets and new channels is not simply a question of thinking more broadly. Companies have to think imaginatively. If the right channels don't exist, the manufacturer may have to invent them. Daewoo's entry into the British car market offers a good example. Daewoo created a radical channel approach to meet fundamental customer needs not satisfied effectively by the existing channel. It started the process with an extensive market research campaign about what customers wanted from a new car company. The campaign was conducted with a toll-free telephone number and a promotion for two hundred free one-year test drives. The result was a database of 200,000 target customers.

The important message from this exercise was that the company started with the customer and the customer's concerns

| COMPANY | **Daewoo Group** | |
|---|---|---|
| Subsidiaries include | Daewoo Motor<br>Daewoo Securities Co., Ltd.<br>Daewoo Electronics | |
| **ADDRESS** | 541 Namdaemunno 5-ga, Chung-gu, Seoul, Korea<br>Phone: +82-2-759-2114   Fax: +82-2-753-9489<br><br>URL: http://www.daewoo.com | |
| **BUSINESS** | Motor vehicles and parts | |
| **STATISTICS** | Employees | 1997   265,044 |
| | Annual sales (mil) | 1997   $71,526 |
| | Annual results<br>Net income (mil) | 1997   $527 |
| | Other facts | Daewoo Group has more than thirty domestic companies and about four hundred foreign subsidiaries. |

and complaints. The actual Daewoo product was not mentioned at this stage. Instead, the company tapped into the residue of ill feeling among consumers. Daewoo found that, consistent with the J.D. Power research in the United States, U.K. customers were not happy with the current system. In particular, they disliked how they were treated when buying a car. They also didn't like the after-sales service they received. In effect, Daewoo positioned itself as the customer's ally.

Daewoo recognized the inherent dealer–manufacturer conflicts of interest and decided that a conventional franchise dealer network would not achieve the desired results. At the same time, it understood the differing economics of the various channel functions and, in response, built a three-tier channel:

- 30 flagship, wholly owned car sales outlets that neither provide service nor sell used cars
- 100 secondary sites, also wholly owned, that sell new cars, perform service, and also sell used cars
- 136 tertiary service sites located at an independent chain of parts and service facilities, Halfords, but staffed by Daewoo personnel

Daewoo's customer understanding helped design every element of the sales and ownership experience so as to maximize satisfaction and provide a consistent brand image. The company consciously sought to establish and maintain direct relationships with customers, without any confusion about who should drive satisfaction and loyalty—the channel or the manufacturer. Daewoo's approach resulted early on in unprecedented success for a new entrant in the United Kingdom, in terms of brand recognition, consumer consideration of the product, and actual market share.

*Channels by Daewoo*

- Start with customers, not products
- Use customer information to create your channels
- Build from the weaknesses of competing channels
- Necessity is the mother of invention

The new competitors were mostly assemblers who competed on their ability to design in the latest components and features, to develop strong channel positions, and, increasingly, to provide good customer service. Some of the biggest winners in this phase of the industry evolution were not the initial pioneers but newcomers that built powerful positions—Compaq, Packard Bell, HP, DEC. Of note is the way the market began to segment, with various players succeeding in different parts of the market, some serving corporate accounts, others supplying specific industry niches or the home market.

Not surprisingly, competitive pressures increased for these assemblers, and the industry then experienced some shakeout. For large portions of the market, economies of scale became much more important in areas such as product development, marketing, purchasing, and customer service investments. Competitors had to relentlessly wring costs out of every element of the value chain to survive. More and more, components were bought from the same suppliers and the same low-cost subcontractors provided board stuffing or even, in some cases, final assembly. The next phase of the industry evolution intensified the competitive pressures on the surviving assemblers selling through retail channels. Just as the original assemblers had capitalized on the weaknesses of the initial direct sales approach, new players adopted another channel that capitalized on the assemblers' weaknesses—a totally new direct-sales approach unlike the industry's initial direct model. This model is restructuring the industry today, creating new winners partly at the expense of the previous generation of high-flyers.

## Beyond PCs to the World

Parallels exist between the PC and the automotive industries (increasingly undifferentiated product offering with service and support growing in importance, inefficiencies in distribution channels, trend toward more direct marketing models and accelerating influence of the Internet, and thin margins in new product sales), and there are interesting lessons to be learned from the PC experience.

## Channel Champions: Directly from Dell

Most prominent among the new direct marketers has been Dell. First using telephone sales and more recently the Internet, Dell bypasses retailers to target corporate accounts by means of dedicated, cross-functional account teams for large accounts and low-cost support for smaller accounts. Dell foresaw the growing sophistication and specific customer service needs of these accounts and the economic advantage of a direct model. Both understanding the needs of a large number of individual accounts and tailoring products to meet their specific requirements can be accomplished not only more cheaply but more effectively without a middleman. The result is "mass customization" as opposed to the traditional method of broad market segmentation. After-sales support can be provided by the corporate customers themselves, by Dell (for example, by pre-loading customer-specific software), or by a third party (for example, through partnerships with EDS and Wang).

| COMPANY | **Dell Computer Corporation** | |
| --- | --- | --- |
| ADDRESS | One Dell Way, Round Rock TX 786682–2244 USA<br>Phone: 512–338–4400   Fax: 512–728–3653<br><br>URL: http://www.dell.com | |
| BUSINESS | Computers, office equipment | |
| STATISTICS | Employees | 1998   16,000 |
| | Annual sales (mil) | 1998* $18,243 |
| | Annual results (mil) | 1998* $2,046 |
| | Other facts | World's #1 direct-sale computer vendor. The company's Web site is expected to transact half of Dell's transactions by the year 2000. |

*Fiscal year ending February 26, 1999.

Channel Champions: Directly from Dell (continued)

The efficiencies of Dell's model are not just manifested in the elimination of intermediary value added. Making to order greatly reduces working capital costs, and the direct access to customers facilitates better product design, inventory management, and customer service. In addition, Dell is noted for execution excellence.

Dell's success is no secret. Dell has been growing at over 50 percent for the last few years. In comparison, number one Compaq has been growing at under 20 percent. In terms of market share Dell is now closing in on Compaq in the United States (14.1 percent versus 15.8 percent in the third quarter of 1998) and is number two in worldwide share behind Compaq.[5] Dell may well end up having the best-performing stock of the decade. Dell's market capitalization stands at $99 billion versus $75 billion and $169 billion for Compaq and IBM, respectively.

Compaq, among others selling through channels, is scrambling to match Dell's advantages. It has instituted build-to-order programs in an effort to emulate Dell but still sells through intermediaries. Given its heavy dependence on resellers, Compaq finds it extraordinarily difficult to bypass them and therefore to best Dell, at least for now. Ultimately, it may well have to abandon the reseller approach for the direct model that has become so successful.

Gateway, another PC maker with a direct-marketing model, focuses on the home consumer market, in contrast to Dell's corporate and institutional strength. Gateway, with about half the market share of Dell, is rolling out its "Country Stores" to

First, direct end customer knowledge is an invaluable tool in developing the right products and services to truly satisfy customer needs and move away from the "product push" approach. Second, major efficiency and effectiveness gains (beyond just savings in dealer costs) can be realized from a manufacturer-direct model. Third, a market-segment-focused approach is valuable in a maturing market. Fourth, a capable company pioneering a better business model can reap large first-mover provide potential customers with a physical site to learn about products in person—the equivalent of a car showroom and test drive. Once a customer makes a choice, fulfillment is handled with a direct system; the Country Stores do not carry inventory.

The ability to match individual end consumer needs with a highly customized product in a cost-effective manner is a real source of sustained competitive advantage for Dell.

*Channels by Dell*

- Direct knowledge of the end consumer builds a satisfied customer base—increasing Dell's brand strength, lowering customer acquisition costs, and boosting customer loyalty.
- Elimination of the retail channel saves on dealer margins—selling costs reduced from 12 percent to between 4 percent and 6 percent of revenue.
- Make-to-order with just-in-time delivery and direct billing decreases working capital costs (no finished goods, low obsolescence, receivables with high credit rating, receivables received before payables paid).
- Feeding customer requirements directly into the production process shortens delivery lead times, and ready-to-boot systems lower start-up time for buyers.
- Low-cost infrastructure and streamlined customer acquisition model facilitate expansion into other markets.
- An involved, empowered, and motivated workforce improves customer satisfaction.

advantages and the benefits can be huge. In fact, it seems the ultimate leader in each phase of the PC industry will be a newcomer. Fifth, either ignoring a new competitive business model or partial attempts to emulate it while protecting the existing business system (as Compaq and others are trying to do with their retailers) can be dangerous to the health of the incumbents.

# Chapter 10
# The One-to-One Advantage

So what's different about the Internet?

The Internet is not the first time that electronic channels have been tried. Previous attempts to create interactive channels have been expensive flops. Walter S. Baer, a senior policy analyst in RAND's Science and Technology division, has charted the history of electronic commerce over the past twenty years.[1] Baer points out that the technologies for electronic home services have actually been around much longer than most people realize. Television was developed in the 1920s, and videophones were on display at the New York World's Fair in 1939. But it wasn't until the 1970s that the growth of cable TV in the United States provoked real interest in the concept of the "wired nation."

In the 1970s, videotext (Viewdata) and teletext (Ceefax) started up in the United Kingdom. In the 1980s, the French government invested heavily in the Minitel service. More recently, U.S. companies have once again pushed the idea of interactive home services including the Full Network—a service that could offer two-way video, audio, and data into the home.

Throughout the largely unprofitable history of electronic commerce, Baer points out, the sorts of service on offer have remained surprisingly similar. Typically these are:

- News and sports information
- Feature information (travel, recipes, and so on)
- Interactive education
- Home shopping
- Banking and financial services
- Ticket ordering (entertainment and travel)
- Interactive games
- Video-on-demand and pay-per-view (for live events)
- Electronic mail and chat services

If the list looks familiar it is because these are the areas that are now being touted as the Internet services of the future.

Given the history, a cynic would take talk of electronic channels' revolutionizing business with a pinch of salt. However, it's hard to imagine that the Internet will not break the losing streak.

The Internet itself has been around for more than two decades. It existed for twenty years for government and military use, and then academic research. Expansion into the commercial market did not start until well into the 1990s. It wasn't until about 1995 that home use really took off. It is that development that is getting businesspeople excited.

As Baer confirms: "Despite obvious over-hyping, there are several reasons for viewing today's developments around the Internet as different:

- More households are buying personal computers
- Internet growth to date has astounded almost everyone: as with all communication products, success breeds success
- Electronic mail usage is broadening
- The World Wide Web is also becoming more popular and easier to use
- Web advertising is expanding rapidly
- Electronic commerce."

In reality, achieving critical mass may well be the factor that finally allows electronic commerce to take off. Taking Baer's first two points, for instance, it is possible to see how fast the Internet is gathering speed.

More home PCs: In 1983, only 9 percent of U.S. households had PCs; this rose to 18 percent in 1989, 27 percent in 1993, and 42 percent in 1997. (In the United Kingdom, according to government figures, 29 percent of households had a PC in 1997.)

What is also significant is that the majority of household PCs in 1983 would have been used for games and other low-end applications, with fewer than 0.5 percent connected to networks. By late 1997, at least half of all household PCs in America had modems and were network capable.

Although Internet usage is notoriously difficult to measure, the best estimates suggest that there are more than sixteen million computers hooked onto the Internet worldwide (probably much more, by the time the estimate goes to press). And this figure does not include the computers behind the firewalls created by most corporations, which would account for many more. That's a great many points of contact, or windows onto the Net. Estimates from Nielsen Media Research suggest that as many as one in four American adults—that's to say fifty million people—are now Internet users.

The growth rate in Internet users, which is probably a more reliable indicator as it compares like with like, has been 100 percent per year for the past five years. This would suggest that between 18 percent and 20 percent of U.S. adults now have regular access to the Internet.

The number of people using the Internet continues to grow at a staggering rate. Many of those who have worked in this area for some time have been amazed by consumer acceptance and use. One survey estimated that 20 percent of new car purchases involve some consultation with the Internet. Yet despite the risks involved with heavy investment in electronic channels, Shikhar Ghosh, chairman and cofounder of Open Market, an Internet-commerce software company, says companies simply cannot afford to ignore the Internet altogether. At the very least, he says, managers "need to understand the opportunities available to them and recognize how their companies may be vulnerable if rivals seize those opportunities first."[2]

Research carried out at London Business School suggests that by the year 2007, in North America and Europe the following percentages of total sales will be on-line in some fashion:

- 10 percent for retail, banks, travel agents, airlines, and mail order clothing firms
- 30 percent for music, books, and newspapers
- 15 percent for groceries
- 10 percent for cars and white goods[3]

E-commerce is already redrawing the corporate map. It has spawned business models that simply could not have existed even a few years ago.

# E-Channels

For all the talk about e-commerce, surprisingly little has been written about how to manage the move from traditional business to Internet-based business. E-channels are no magic bullet. With a few glorious exceptions, most companies are still struggling to create profitable business models based on the Internet. As is so often the case, the practice lags some way behind the hype.

Shikhar Ghosh sums up the situation: "The Internet is fast becoming an important new channel for commerce in a range of businesses—much faster than anyone would have predicted two years ago. But determining how to take advantage of the opportunities this new channel is creating will not be easy for most executives, especially those in large, well-established companies."[4]

The Internet is an exciting new frontier. It opens up new business vistas. But it would be foolhardy to assume it is an easy option. Far from it. Our work in this area suggests that e-channels are actually more difficult to operate effectively than traditional channels. The point is that they are worth investing serious time and effort in because they are potentially so powerful. At present, however, many companies are throwing money at the issue in the blind hope that it will transform their

## Channel Champions: Books in Cyberspace

The best-known of these new businesses is Amazon.com. The first books ordered through Amazon were dispatched in the fall of 1994 (personally packed by founder Jeff Bezos and his wife); in 1997 Amazon sold its one millionth book. In 1997, sales approached $148 million, an eightfold increase year on year.

Already, it is proving difficult to predict where this exciting new channel will take business. For example, the original model for Amazon.com was to provide the world's largest bookshop with 2.5 million volumes available. (Most competitors don't come close to this level; see Exhibit 10.1.) But it quickly found that it was actually selling information as much as books. Today, for example, Amazon ("the toast of cyberspace," according to the *Financial Times*) will send customers an e-mail message every time a new book comes out on a subject in which they have registered an interest. That information also helps the company better understand its customers and target its marketing.

| COMPANY | **Amazon.com, Inc.** | |
| --- | --- | --- |
| **ADDRESS** | 1516 Second Avenue, Seattle WA 98101<br>Phone: 206–622–2335   Fax: 206–622–2405<br><br>URL: http://www.amazon.com | |
| **BUSINESS** | Specialty retail—books, music, videos on-line. | |
| **STATISTICS** | Employees | 1997   614 |
| | Annual sales (mil) | 1998   $610.0 |
| | Annual results (mil) | 1998   ($124.5) |
| | Other facts | Amazon.com sells 1.5 million in-print titles and 1 million out-of-print titles via the Internet. |

## Channel Champions: Books in Cyberspace (continued)

### Exhibit 10.1   The World's Largest On-Line Bookstores

| Bookstore | Country | Deliverable Titles (million) |
|---|---|---|
| Amazon.com | United States | 2.5 |
| Alt.bookstore | United States | 2.0 |
| Abiszet Bucherservice | Germany | 1.3 |
| Foyles | United Kingdom | 1.0 |
| Barnes & Noble | United States | 1.0 |
| The Co-op Bookshop | Australia | 1.0 |
| Libro Web | Spain | 1.0 |
| Internet Bookshop IBS | United Kingdom | 0.92 |
| J.F. Lehmanns | Germany | 0.75 |
| Book Stacks Unlimited | United States | 0.5 |

*Source:* Jonathan Bowen, Oxford University Computing Laboratory

The site also encourages "chat" among its users as part of its service. To encourage discussion, it not only posts book reviews from leading newspapers, it also encourages customers to send in their own reviews, which are published on the Amazon site.

Despite its popularity with consumers, business journalists, and academics, Amazon.com has yet to make a profit. When it does, it may well have to face up to me-too imitators replicating a successful channel. Other pioneers that have invested heavily in Internet services could face similar problems further down the road.

More immediate problems for Amazon.com appear to lie in its diversification into music retailing. This has already caused it trouble. Its book retailing model does not quite fit—Bezos has said that he doesn't understand music, which is driven by current hits, teenagers who don't have credit cards, and an array of local promotions.

*Channels by Amazon.com*

- Information is a service even if it is not your business.
- Gather information from customers.
- Use logistics to achieve convenience.

business overnight. Worse still, many are simply running scared that their competitors will crack the e-channel code before they do.

In some sectors the development of e-channels is reminiscent of the Space Race. In the 1950s and 1960s, both the United States and the Soviet Union pumped money into their space programs because each feared the other would beat it to the punch.

E-channels will change whole industries. It will not be by luck, however, but by effective channel management. There are lessons to be learned from the implementation of IT in the 1980s. The companies that used IT to best effect then were those that approached it with a clear idea of what they wanted to achieve.

It's a point made in a recent article in *Fast Company*.[5] The question that enlightened organizations asked in the 1980s was, What business are we in? In the early 1990s, that changed as companies such as Dell began asking, What is the best business model? Today, the question is changing yet again. Now it is, What can e-commerce do for the customer? In reality, it is all about applying the new technology to the right part of the business. The point is that it is no good simply creating e-channels for the sake of it. Digital technology is most effective when it is linked to a specific strategic goal.

So, for example, when Intel invested $300 million in CAD/CAM technology in 1986, it did so to achieve a clear objective. CAD/CAM was the digital answer to a purely competitive question: How could Intel create a two-year lead over its competitors? Becoming more digital in the design and production of microchips was key to improving competitive advantage.

Similarly, at about the same time, Wal-Mart invested roughly the same amount on digital technology to support a different business goal, digitizing its logistics system. By installing sophisticated communications and stock management systems to provide real-time sales-and-ordering information, the company moved from atoms to bits. As a result, the retailer outperformed its competitors.

These two companies were in the vanguard of the digital revolution. The impact of their decisions is clear for all to see. Other companies are making investments today that will create competitive advantage in the future. The hard part is figuring out where the new technology can make the most difference. The same rigor should be applied to e-channels.

E-channels can be leveraged by companies at three different levels.

- As information platforms
- As transaction platforms
- As platforms for building and managing the customer relationship

The impact on the business increases as you move up the levels. Currently, most companies primarily use e-channels as information platforms, although, increasingly, they are experimenting with innovative ways to use them as transaction platforms and to build more sophisticated customer relationships.

The progression from information to relationship platform is a logical one. It might be tempting to try to jump to the third level and skip the first two, but in most cases, this is unlikely to be successful.

In time—as customers become more comfortable with e-commerce—this may be possible, but for the time being it is more sensible to roll out e-channels one level at a time. The most effective e-channels involve an evolution from low-value to high-value platforms.

The point is that customers demand a quality information platform before they are prepared to enter into electronic transactions. If you visit a Web site that performs poorly at the basic tasks of providing information, you are hardly encouraged to be confident of its ability to perform transactions. The customer must be satisfied at both of these levels before being willing to enter into a meaningful dialogue or electronic relationship. Get it right at the first level and you can then proceed to the other two. That doesn't mean the three levels cannot be developed simultaneously. It simply suggests that effective roll-out builds on the initial competence.

The evolution of technology—basically the bandwidth—also favors this approach. As the Internet becomes faster and more able to deliver high-quality images and more personalized service, so the business opportunities increase.

Companies that attempt to go straight to the high-impact third level risk being let down by the technology. There is evidence to suggest that once customers have had a bad e-channel experience they are less willing to give it another try. The customers neither know nor care what went wrong, they just know they got a poor response from the company and therefore they regard the company as a poor risk. A customer who browses a Web site and takes the time to complete a marketing questionnaire finds it impressive if that feedback informs the marketing material the company sends out—and ludicrous if it doesn't. Customers aren't interested in technological failures, only in results.

## Level 1: Informational Platform

E-channels are already used widely as informational platforms. Technological improvements mean that their functionality is rapidly improving. Today, such channels are used to provide customers with instant information on product specifications and features. They also allow the potential buyer to customize features and options—even colors—to make a personalized purchase decision.

For example, Dell and Gateway both have Web sites that allow the customer to build a PC to personal specifications from a list of off-the-shelf components. The site automatically adjusts the price. In future, smart interfaces—which reconfigure to meet individual customer requirements—and higher Internet speeds will make this increasingly powerful.

## Level 2: Transaction Platform

At the second level, e-channels provide additional information and a mechanism for making transactions. Already, such systems are used to provide quotations, place orders, check availability, and access additional services—such as financing or insurance. A growing number of companies, particularly in the IT sector, are already selling to other businesses successfully through electronic channels using the Web. Cisco Systems now sells over $2 billion a year on the Web.

The stumbling block here remains the security of payment. However, this is unlikely to present a serious problem to the future development of e-channels. Some customers will be more comfortable with a parallel payment channel, preferring to place their orders electronically but pay by more traditional means. Increasingly, however, credit cards and other instant payment methods mean that the e-channel can provide a complete system for transactions. Amazon.com, for one, has shown that this is a workable model.

## Level 3: Platform for Managing Customer Relationships

This level incorporates the first two levels. It is here that e-channels have the most potential impact. By creating an ongoing dialogue with customers they theoretically offer a way to market to segments of one. To date, however, the practice is a long way behind the theory. Some companies are experimenting at this level through interactive entertainment, special offers targeted at customer segments, and even tie-ins with other products. So, for example, Internet service providers and magazines use information push technology to deliver regular updates and advance information via e-mail. Over time, this practice will become more widespread.

The key attribute of the e-channel is its ability to push as well as pull information. Push too much information and the customer will become irritated and pull the plug. At present, much of the discussion about e-commerce focuses on providing information to customers. Properly managed, the e-channel is not just a tool for consumer communication, it can enhance each element of the value chain. For example, in the case of a car manufacturer, e-channels can have a major impact on innovation, demand, and delivery. The key to effectiveness, however, lies in managing the flow of information.

In the area of innovation and development, e-channels can be used by the company to improve and speed up the development process, transmitting important data from, say, the marketing department to R&D. The same data can then be used to support and enhance project management, ensuring an improved time to market. Crucially, e-channels can also facilitate the transfer of knowledge between different parts of the organization. If, for example, one development team makes a technical breakthrough that can speed up development in other teams, or can be built into the marketing of other products, other teams can quickly take advantage of the new insight.

At a later stage, e-channels can be used to stimulate demand by pushing information and offers to selected customers. This results in improved customer segmentation, more targeted promotions, and more personalized customer care. For instance, if one group of customers has expressed an interest in a prospective new service or option while another has shown none, this information can be used to target the people who want the service without bothering those who don't. It also means it can be offered to different customers at a price level that corresponds to the value they attach to it. Perhaps the new offering is a monthly valeting service. The logistics of providing the service—plus the level of service—can be accurately targeted.

Finally, the e-channel has other important benefits when it is used as a delivery mechanism. It can create a personalized service bundle for individual customers. It can also improve the performance of the company in the areas of procurement, logistics, manufacture, and distribution.

# One-to-One Loyalty

As the flourishing warfare in cyberspace illustrates, segments are becoming ever more fragmented, ever smaller.

Visit the flagship Levi's store in London's Regent Street and you can climb the stairs and order a pair of customized jeans. Details are fed into a computer and then to Belgium where the jeans are made. They arrive three weeks later complete with a personalized bar code to make reordering straightforward. The ultimate mass-marketed product is now available in customized form. This is mass customization in its purest form.

Mass customization tends to be thought of as one-off product differentiation. It is Burger King's "Have it your way" campaign. It offers dramatically increased variety at the same or lower cost and developed in response to increasing fragmentation of consumer preferences. Most examples focus on the clever use of manufacturing in mass customization of products—such as Levi's made-to-order jeans and Motorola's pagers—or the clever use of databases in mass customization of services. It is usually understood as a product-based concept.

As we have noted, product-based differentiation is diminishing in importance and value. So the danger with customizing products en masse is that it does not necessarily add value to the channel. McDonald's, for example, trumpets its "Made for you" system of preparation. Announcing its introduction, then chairman and CEO Michael Quinlan said, "The most important benefit to customers will be fresher, hotter food, served fast. Restaurant managers and crew will benefit from an easy-to-use system that takes the stress and guesswork out of delivering great-tasting food."[6] The value-added service, it appears, is to give customers what they should already have been receiving—and to make life better for McDonald's staff.

But what if you regard customization as a channel-based concept? Why not customize the add-on services as well as, or rather than, the product? Indeed, mass customization is actually easier—and cheaper—in the service business. Customizing the wrap-around services can be more valuable than customizing the product. The challenge is to keep products intact while changing associated services. This is the smart way to do customization.

Organizations like Disney and Marriott have turned service into a replicable but flexible commodity that can be managed through a variety of channels. Look at Ritz Carlton, which has become the Lexus of hotels. It has managed to bring all of the operational efficiency of the Marriott hotel empire and to deliver it effectively to the highest segment of the market.

True customer care improvement requires knowledge of service-based, channel-driven needs. This understanding must typically be built from scratch. Facts and data are usually required to supplement, or counter, existing biases and intuition, and understanding the customer's underlying economic dynamics is crucial. It is also essential to objectively assess the inevitable costs versus the benefits. The insights about customer service requirements must clearly uncover specific variations across non-homogeneous groupings. The purpose of segmentation in this context is to identify sets of customers whose key drivers of value differ so that solutions can be designed accordingly.

Consider the customized customer care program used by GE's electrical distribution products unit. One part of this business makes circuit breakers and panel boards for new or retrofitted commercial and industrial buildings. Contractors purchase the products from electrical distributors. They also receive a variety of services directly from the manufacturer that depend on the size and type of job, since the products are often specified, priced, and built for a particular job.

The economics of the contracting business are such that delays in receiving materials at the job site are extremely costly. Labor and equipment costs, possible completion deadline penalties, and subsequent delays for other contractors affect the economic equation. So the primary need of all contractors is on-time delivery.

However, the secondary need varies by type of contractor or type of job. For many small projects, "quote responsiveness" is very nearly as important as on-time delivery. Unlike large jobs that have a long, complex bidding and quoting process, small jobs tend to have a short fuse and can be won or lost based on the contractor's ability to quote quickly.

GE recognized this distinction and developed an easy-to-use, PC-based quoting system for small jobs that the distributor can use instead of having the manufacturer involved, as in the process for large jobs. Consequently, GE's quote time is recognized as faster than that of its three major competitors, a distinction that has given GE a significantly greater share in this targeted and higher-margin portion of the market.

## One-to-One Channels

Smart use of channels can play an important role in mass customization of products and the service bundles surrounding them.

Take the example of the office supplies company Viking Direct. Viking sells a range of stationery and other office consumables. To a large extent its products are commodities—from the user's point of view, one brand of staples, fax paper, or computer disks is pretty similar to another. Yet in the space of just fourteen years, Viking has grown from a revenue of $15 million to $1.3 billion. How, then, is Viking different from the competition?

Along with keen pricing, the company explicitly recognizes that the delivery channel it operates with the consumer is all important. What really matters is that the office supplies are there when needed. Viking therefore guarantees 99 percent of deliveries on the same day if orders are placed early enough.

But the company has also gone one step further down the channel management road. By collating information about orders and inquiries it is able to create an individualized profile of each customer. This information is used to generate a personalized catalog for a market segment of one.

The catalog even has the customer's name on the cover. It only includes office supplies that the customer is interested in purchasing. The result, Viking says, is almost a 100 percent response rate. In other words, virtually every catalog sent out results in an order being placed. In this case it isn't the product that is customized but the menu of choices.

In effect, what the company is doing is providing a customized channel for each of its profiled customers. Yet the products it sells have little to differentiate them. Other companies could do the same. Think about a car company that understands the features and service elements you as a customer want and offers to build your perfect car? Or a restaurant that offers you a menu of your favorite dishes?

Think about the savings involved with that sort of targeted mail shot. And all because the company recognizes the power of channel management. Best of all, the individual products themselves remain untouched—uncustomized. It doesn't matter whether the box of staples is bought by customer A from his personalized catalog or by customer Z from hers. It is the catalog—a service—that is tailored, not the inventory.

Direct sales computer companies such as Dell and Gateway provide another example of mass customization through channel management. Both companies provide interactive Web sites. Special deals involving bundled systems are trailed through advertising in the national press. They state a price for a given specification, but also encourage customers to "build their own spec" using the interactive Web site.

Customers who visit the Gateway or Dell Web sites can entertain themselves for hours by upgrading the individual components of the system without taking up the time of a sales assistant. In each case, by clicking on options the window shopper can instantly see the price difference a small alteration to the spec will make. Finally, when ready to make a purchase, the customer can order either on-line with a credit card or over the telephone.

What the companies hold as inventory is limited to component parts. Complete systems are built only when an order has been received, thus completely avoiding rework. To encourage customers to use the Internet channel, Gateway also offers additional benefits to customers who order via the "system builder" on its Web site. By accessing the service they can qualify for free upgrades and other special offers not available to those purchasing through other channels.

In fact, Gateway has created a range of different channels for its customers, recognizing that their purchasing patterns and preferences vary. Today, the company operates a telephone sales and information channel and a Web site sales and information channel. It also provides showrooms where customers can walk in and touch the product and talk to Gateway employees (although purchases have to be made through one of the other channels). In addition, it communicates with customers via extensive advertising in specialized computer magazines and the national press.

What all these channels have in common is that they involve a direct relationship with the company with no middleman. The technology enables companies to bypass others in the value chain. For example, a book publisher could use the Net to bypass book retailers by selling directly to consumers. And the advantage works in both directions—by ordering parts directly via the Internet, GE estimates it will shave $500 million to $700 million off its purchasing costs over three years and reduce purchasing cycle times by as much as 50 percent. Within five years, GE anticipates it will purchase almost everything it buys through its Web-based bidding system. GE started its Trading Process Network as a means of electronic data interchange, and then shifted it to the Internet. GE purchases via this system now run well over $1 billion a year. Transaction costs are lower, the range of potential suppliers is wider (which keeps prices down), and tender responses are faster. So successful has the system been that the company has now made it available to other firms for a fee.

Gateway does not manufacture all its own components, buying in from other leading suppliers such as Toshiba and Intel, but it has successfully retained control over both the quality of its products and the relationship with its customers. Relationships are everything. They are the end product of successful channel management.

## In the End Is the Beginning

The channel management process we have outlined in this book is never ending. Learnings lead into fresh customer insights, new segments, and the ceaseless evolution of new channels.

Once again, if you want inspiration look at Dell. As we write, it is moving its understanding of channels forward. It has announced an on-line store that will sell thirty thousand computer-related products as well as Dell PCs. One estimate was that the new feature could boost visits to the company's Web site by 20 percent over the first six months of operation. Estimates of Dell's daily Internet sales now stand at $14 million. Grounds for complacency, some would say. Not at Dell, where fear of losing customers to competitors looms large. "They might decide to buy their next PC at somebodyelse.com," said Michael Dell.[7] Proactively managing channels and developing new ones is the way to stay ahead.

# Notes

**Preface**

1. Margetta, Joan, "The Power of Virtual Integration," *Harvard Business Review,* Mar./Apr. 1998.

**Chapter 1**

1. Hebe, James, speech to American Truck Dealers Convention, 8 Apr. 1995.
2. Despite growing restaurant numbers by 50 percent, McDonald's has lost 2 percent market share in fast food sales. As we write, McDonald's has announced a $190 million plan to alter kitchen equipment in all of its 12,380 U.S. outlets. The aim is to "individualize" McDonald's burgers. Unfortunately for McDonald's, however, concentrating on the product plays into the hands of Burger King. As second in the market, Burger King has nothing to lose and a great deal to gain through product promotions like National Free Fry Day—giving everyone a free portion of fries cooked to a new formula.
3. Of course, as we will see, substantial, sustainable differentiation in terms of basic product values that the supplier directly controls—such as functionality, quality, or even styling—is harder to come by. Attributes can provide more powerful sources of differentiation—such as an emotional bond between the customer and the product.
4. Authers, John, "Every Expense Pared," *Financial Times,* 10 Nov. 1997.
5. *U.S. Automotive News,* 16 Nov. 1998.

6. The subtext was that though P&G was ahead with its product, at the time it didn't understand well enough how to market beauty care products. To its credit (and through the acquisition of companies with cosmetic businesses) it quickly learned the lesson.

7. From one product generation to the next, customers' perceptions of the industry's range of performance in the two primary product-driven drivers of satisfaction shrank sharply. At the same time, the industry's average satisfaction level was increasing on both dimensions.

8. On 2 April 1993, Philip Morris cut the price of its branded cigarettes (including Marlboro) by 25 percent. Marlboro Friday, as it was known, marked a watershed in brand management. No longer could a premium brand sit tight and reap rewards. It had to fight for every sale.

   This was followed by Diaper Tuesday in November 1994, when P&G reduced the price of its Luvs brand by 11 percent—despite rapidly increasing raw material prices—in an effort to get ahead in the fiercely competitive diaper market.

   The Soap Wars were a 1994 battle between P&G and Unilever in Europe. The starting point was Unilever's launch of the Persil Power detergent. P&G countered with claims that the new detergent damaged clothing. A public relations battle followed. In 1995, Unilever announced that it was writing off £57 million of stock thanks to the Soap Wars.

9. McGregor, Alexander, "Torn in the USA?" *Financial Times,* How to Spend It Supplement, May 1998.

## Chapter 2

1. Fites, Donald V., "Make Your Dealers Partners," *Harvard Business Review,* Mar.-Apr. 1996.

2. "Wal-Mart MasterCard from Chase Reaches 1 Million Accounts," *Business Wire,* 7 Aug. 1997.

3. Taylor, Paul, "Key Role for Business Intelligence," *Financial Times,* 1 Apr. 1998.

4. Rifkin, Glen, "How Snap-on Tools Ratchets Its Brand," *Strategy & Business,* 1st Quarter 1998.

5. Tomkins, Richard, "Wackiness on the Wing," *Financial Times,* 7 May 1998.

6. Paraphrased from Leonard, Dorothy, *Wellsprings of Knowledge,* Boston: Harvard Business School Press, 1998.

7. Rayport, Jeffrey F., and John J. Sviokla, "Exploiting the Virtual Value Chain," *Harvard Business Review,* Nov.-Dec. 1995.

8. Reynolds, Jonathan, "Mastering Global Business, Pt 7," *Financial Times,* 13 May 1998.

9. "Wal-Mart Selects NCR to Expand World's Largest Commercial Database Solution," *Business Wire,* 3 May 1996.
10. Taylor, Paul, "Making Close Links with Shoppers," *Financial Times,* 17 Mar. 1998.
11. Stedman, Craig, "Wal-Mart Mines for Forecasts," *Computer World,* 26 May 1997.
12. Taylor, Paul, "Key Role for Business Intelligence," *Financial Times,* 1 Apr. 1998.
13. Dearlove, Des, "Cherry Picking Top Talent," *Financial Times,* 16 Nov. 1994.
14. "7-Eleven Operators Resist System to Monitor Managers," *Wall Street Journal,* 16 June 1997.
15. Hutton, Bethan, "Japan's 7–Eleven Sets Store by Computer Links," *Financial Times,* 17 Mar. 1998.
16. Margetta, Joan, "The Power of Virtual Integration," *Harvard Business Review,* Mar.-Apr. 1998.
17. Margetta, "The Power of Virtual Integration."
18. Crainer, Stuart, "In Search of Oink," *Management Review,* Jan. 1999.
19. Crainer, "In Search of Oink."
20. King, Jenny, "One-Price Sellers Find Niche in Some Markets," *Automotive News,* 27 Jan. 1997.
21. McGahan, Anita M., and Suzanne C. Purdy, "Saturn Corporation in 1996," Harvard Business School case study 9–797–052 Copyright © 1996 by the President and Fellows of Harvard College.

## Chapter 3

1. P.Four Consulting, "What Makes Successful Businesses Successful?" London, 1997.
2. Chernatony, Leslie de, and Francesca Dall'Olmo Riley, "Branding in the Service Sector," Mastering Global Management, *Financial Times,* Sept. 1997.
3. *Analyst Report,* 21 Apr. 1997.
4. Interview with Jeff Bennet, Booz·Allen & Hamilton partner, Cleveland.
5. Uncles, Mark, "Making Loyalty Work," *Address,* Jan. 1996.
6. "Don't Get Left on the Shelf," *Economist,* 2 July 1994.
7. Cuneo, Alice, "Marketer of the Year: The Gap," *Fortune,* Dec. 1997.
8. Clutterbuck, David, and Walter Goldsmith, *The Winning Streak II,* London: Orion, 1997.

## Chapter 4

1. Crainer, Stuart, *The Ultimate Book of Business Quotations,* New York: AMACOM, 1998.

2. Pinnell, Raoul, "Opinion," *Address,* Summer 1996.
3. Hill, Sam, David Newkirk, and Wayne Henderson, "Dismantling the Brandocracy," *Strategy & Business,* 4th Quarter 1995.
4. Hollinger, Peggy, "Super Market Success," *New World,* Jan. 1998.
5. "Republic Industries Launches Far-Reaching Customer Initiatives in Denver," *Business Wire,* 23 Sept. 1998. Republic Industries changed its corporate name to AutoNation shortly before this book went to press.

## Chapter 5

1. Crainer, Stuart, *The Ultimate Book of Business Quotations,* New York: AMACOM, 1998.
2. Feder, Barnaby J., "McDonald's Finds There's Still Plenty of Room to Grow," *New York Times,* 9 Jan. 1994.
3. Kramer, Louise, "McDonald's Develops Own C-Store Concept," *Nations Restaurant News,* 28 Aug. 1995.
4. "Fast Foods Give Passengers a Fast Break," *World Airport Week,* 18 June 1996.
5. "McDonald's to Step Up Expansion Plans for Next Few Years," *Nations Restaurant News,* 6 Dec. 1993.
6. Kramer, "McDonald's Develops Own C-Store Concept."
7. Kramer, "McDonald's Develops Own C-Store Concept."

## Chapter 6

1. Emerson, Ralph W. *Essays* (First Series), 1841.

## Chapter 7

1. Argyris, Chris, *Strategy & Business,* 1st Quarter 1998.
2. Lucier, Charles, Leslie Moeller, and Raymond Held, "10X Value: The Engine Powering Long-Term Returns to Shareholders," *Strategy & Business,* 3rd Quarter 1997.
3. Henkoff, Ronald, "Moving Up by Downscaling," *Fortune,* 9 Aug. 1993.
4. Henkoff, "Moving Up by Downscaling."
5. Interview with Evan Hirsh.

## Chapter 8

1. Crainer, Stuart, *The Ultimate Book of Business Quotations,* New York: AMACOM, 1998.
2. The Sherwin-Williams name is strong with male customers. However, women buy 33 percent of consumer paint, according to the 1996 Paint Consumer Market Research Report, and are the target market for the Martha Stewart line.

3. "Tread Carefully," *Economist,* 6 Feb. 1999.

4. "Jack Welch's Encore," *Business Week,* 28 Oct. 1996.

5. "Jack," *Business Week,* 8 June 1998.

6. Simpson, Peter, "Intelligent Customer Dialogue," *Address,* Summer 1996.

7. "W.W. Grainger Inc. Collaborates with Perot Systems Corp. on Internet Commerce Initiative," *PR Newswire,* 29 Apr. 1998.

## Chapter 9

1. International Management Symposium, London Business School, 11 Nov. 1997.

2. Rayport, Jeffrey, and John Sviokla, "Exploiting the Virtual Value Chain," *Harvard Business Review,* Nov.-Dec. 1995.

3. Hamel, Gary, comments at International Management Symposium, London Business School, 11 Nov. 1997.

4. Kim, W. Chan, and Renee Mauborgne, "Value Innovation: The Strategic Logic of High Growth," *Harvard Business Review,* Jan.-Feb. 1997.

5. International Data Corporation, 1998.

## Chapter 10

1. Baer, Walter S., "Will the Internet Bring Electronic Services to the Home?" *Business Strategy Review,* Spring 1998, *9*(1).

2. Ghosh, Shikhar, "Making Business Sense of the Internet," *Harvard Business Review,* Mar.-Apr. 1998.

3. London Business School, Future Media Project.

4. Ghosh, "Making Business Sense of the Internet."

5. Slywotzky, Adrian, "How Digital Is Your Company?" *Fast Company,* Feb. 1999.

6. Tomkins, Richard, "All Change in McDonald's U.S. Kitchens," *Financial Times,* 27 Mar. 1998.

7. Ramstad, Evan, "Dell Builds an Electronics Superstore on the Web," *Wall Street Journal,* 3 Mar. 1999.

# The Authors

**Steven Wheeler** has fifteen years of consulting experience in channel strategies and management across such industries as automotive, trucking, aftermarket, consumer packaged goods, building products, and industrial companies. He presently leads the automotive activities for Booz·Allen & Hamilton in Europe, based out of the Munich office, and is a member of the Board of Directors of the company.

**Evan Hirsh** is a vice president of Booz·Allen & Hamilton based in the firm's Chicago office. During his twelve years in management consulting, he has worked on a range of assignments for consumer and industrial products companies. He is currently concentrating on helping companies design and implement strategies to win with innovative distribution and marketing approaches.

# Index

# Booz·Allen & Hamilton

**B**ooz·Allen & Hamilton is one of the world's leading international management and technology consulting firms, providing services in strategy, systems, operations, and technology to clients in more than seventy-five countries around the globe.

Founded in 1914, Booz·Allen & Hamilton pioneered the business of management consulting. Today, Booz·Allen has more than nine thousand employees in one hundred offices on six continents with sales exceeding $1.6 billion. Its client base comprises a majority of the world's largest industrial and service corporations, as well as major institutions and government bodies around the world, including most U.S. federal departments and agencies.

Booz·Allen is a private corporation organized into two major business sectors: the Worldwide Commercial Business (WCB) and the Worldwide Technology Business (WTB). WCB clients are primarily major international corporations; WTB generally serves governmental clients both in the United States and abroad.

Booz·Allen helps senior management solve complex problems through its expertise in more than two dozen industries as well as information technology, operations management, and strategic leadership.

Consistent with its position as a business thought leader, Booz·Allen publishes the award-winning quarterly journal, *Strategy & Business,* which reports on the latest developments in global management techniques, competitive tactics, and strategic thinking.

For more information, please visit Booz·Allen's Website at www.bah.com or contact the company at:

Booz·Allen & Hamilton
101 Park Ave.
New York, NY 10178
(212) 697–1900

This *Strategy & Business* book is an excellent business relationship-building tool. By giving this book to your clients, partners, and prospects, you can contribute to their knowledge in a business world where staying current is the only lasting competitive edge. Receive substantial quantity discounts when you place bulk orders. Let us personalize the books with your message.

For quantity discounts and customized orders, contact:

Bernadette Walter
Corporate Sales Manager
Jossey-Bass Publishers
350 Sansome Street
San Francisco, CA 94104–1342
phone: (415) 782–3122
fax: (415) 433–0499
e-mail: bwalter@jbp.com

# CEO spoken here.

# MORE STRATEGY & BUSINESS BOOKS FROM BOOZ•ALLEN & HAMILTON

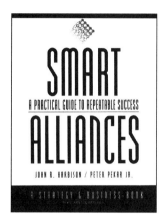

## SMART ALLIANCES
**A Practical Guide to Repeatable Success**
John R. Harbison, Peter Pekar Jr.
Hardcover   208 pages
ISBN 0-7879-4326-6   $35.00

## BALANCED SOURCING
**Cooperation and Competition in Supplier Relationships**
Timothy M. Laseter
Hardcover   288 pages
ISBN 0-7879-4443-2
$40.00

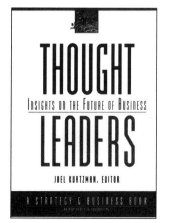

## THOUGHT LEADERS
**Insights on the Future of Business**
Joel Kurtzman, Editor
Hardcover   192 pages
ISBN 0-7879-3903-X   $27.00

**AVAILABLE IN BOOKSTORES OR CALL 800.956.7739**